WHEN LIFE INTERRUPTS LIFE

WHAT DO YOU DO WHEN LIFE DOESN'T GO AS PLANNED?

Maurice Valentine, Th.D.

Copyright © 2024 by Maurice Valentine

All rights reserved. This book or any portion thereof may not be reproduced or used in any manner whatsoever without the express written permission of the publisher except for the use of brief quotations in a book review or scholarly journal.

Scripture quotations taken from The Holy Bible, King James Version, Cambridge, 1769.

Scripture taken from the New King James Version®. Copyright © 1982 by Thomas Nelson. Used by permission. All rights reserved.

Scripture quotations from The ESV® Bible (The Holy Bible, English Standard Version®), copyright © 2001 by Crossway, a publishing ministry of Good News Publishers. Used by permission. All rights reserved.

First Printing: 2024

ISBN (Hardback): 978-1-7372734-2-4
ISBN (Paperback): 978-1-7372734-3-1
ISBN (E-Book): 978-1-7372734-4-8

Library of Congress Control Number: 2022901113

Cover Design by Daneja Graphix LLC
Book Interior Design by Greater Works Enterprises

Greater Works Enterprises
Website: www.greaterworksenterprises.com

DEDICATION

This book is dedicated first and foremost to Salisia Valentine: the strongest woman I know, my Queen, and the love of my life. I also dedicate it to my Father, Mother, and Sisters: Charles, Dora, Ketwana Valentine, and Valisa Brown. My dedication continues to: my Spiritual Parents, Andra and Cynthia Cunningham; my wonderful church family, Life Changing

Christian Center; and a host of family and friends that played a big part during the challenging moments of our lives.

Table of Contents

DEDICATION v

INTRODUCTION 1

CHAPTER I 9
    LIFE INTERRUPTIONS – "THINGS TO COME"

CHAPTER II 26
    GET UP!

CHAPTER III 44
    YET, I AM NOT ALONE

CHAPTER IV 64
    I THOUGHT IT WOULD BE BETTER BY NOW

CHAPTER V 97
    HARD PRESSED BUT NOT DESTROYED

CHAPTER VI 126
    ADDICTION

CHAPTER VII 144
    DEALING WITH DISAPPOINTMENTS

CHAPTER VIII 169
    GET A THERAPIST

CHAPTER IX 189
    LIVE AGAIN

ABOUT THE AUTHOR 208

INTRODUCTION

Disclaimer: This is a transparent account of how my life was interrupted by Diverticulitis. Please know that medications affect people differently. Please consult with your provider before making any changes to your daily regime.

Writing this book has been a significant challenge because I didn't want to revisit some parts of my battle. I have learned that the mind is powerful and can hold moments from our pasts along with their feelings and struggles. I sure didn't want to reawaken those moments of struggle within my life. I truly wanted to leave them alone. Nevertheless, I was able to write this book through much prayer, therapy, and, most of all, God's strength. This book's purpose is to help someone navigate through the uncertainty of life and develop a hope to live and pursue life again. If you're reading this and you're in a place of hopelessness and despair, please hear my heart when I tell you it does get better. When? I can't tell you. It was a lost and unbelievable phrase to me, but one thing I know for sure is that it does get better.

Every person who said that phrase to me, "It will get better," made me extremely mad or bitterly numb. I didn't want to hear that it would get better. I wanted to know when will it get better. The place of uncertainty can be challenging, and hopefully, this book will help you embrace where you are and understand that life may not make any sense at the moment, and that's okay! You're NOT CRAZY! It's called Life! It's not the devil. It's not God getting back at you. It's not karma. It's just called LIFE. Many of us never planned for our lives to shift. We never asked for the surgery, the tragic loss of our loved ones, the divorce, the loss of our job, etc. We thought that we would have the dream job, the ideal marriage, and the longevity of our loved ones, but somehow life happened. What is life? Life is like that line on the EKG machine. The EKG machine is what they use to check the signals from your heart. The machine line is flat when no one connects to the machine, or the attached person has lost his life. But when there is life in the person, the line shows activity by going up and down. That, my friend, is life.

Life is a journey of ups and downs. Life has its good days and bad days. Life sometimes goes as we planned it, and sometimes it doesn't. Life has days of joy and days of pain.

Christ told us in John 10:10 (b), "But I've come, that you might have LIFE and have it more ABUNDANTLY." Unfortunately, we have been taught that this abundant life is a life without ups and downs. Many times someone equates a great life to things they possess. The problem with that is that our possessions can't change the diagnosis. Our possessions can't change whether our child has an addiction or our life experiences interruptions. No, the abundant life that Christ speaks of is not a life without ups and downs but a life with ups and downs that's still full of God's presence and His Peace.

God's peace isn't found just in the great moments like the promotion, the wedding day, or the birth of your child. You can experience it in the struggles of life, the demotions, and, as hard as it is to believe, even in the loss of a loved one. You see, peace isn't in our lives to avoid trials; it's in our lives to help us stand face to face with them. With our fists clenched tight, pain in our hearts, and tears flowing from our eyes, we stand in God's peace. Remember, God could have easily chosen to meet the three Hebrew boys outside the fire; however, He decided to have a prayer conference in the fire. He could have rescued Daniel before being thrown into the lion's den; however, He wanted to meet Daniel in the lion's den. Although it makes sense to have a service with God outside the fire, it's in the fire that the revelation of who God is to us can be made known and received. It's easy to know that God is with us outside of the fire, but it's an even more incredible feeling to know He's with us in the fire.

God has brought my wife and me through many fires, lion's dens, and trials of life. As of this writing, we've been married for fourteen beautiful years, soon to be fifteen, and we have experienced the EKG of life. When we first got married, we had it all planned out. After the first two years of marriage, we would have children, travel, build a ministry, and enjoy life. We have experienced two miscarriages; I've had cancer that altered my life and took away my ability to have children, but I beat it by the grace of God. We had financial battles, including falling behind on the mortgage that almost made us lose our first home. My wife had begun to deal with heart problems, and at one time, she lost her job, which left us with only one income. We had candlelight dinners, not by choice, but because we couldn't afford to pay the light bill. We made the best of every challenge. What we had planned and what we experienced were not the same. However, God was with us. We were and are financially disciplined, but life just happened. When it came to our children's future, we had our kids' names picked out. We had our destinations to travel picked out. A man of God prophesied that we would have ten beautiful children. Boy, did he miss it or what? Or that's what I thought. Although the prophecy didn't go as we desired, and we don't have kids of our own yet, he didn't miss it

> *Through it all, God has brought us through many trials of life*

because we do have 12 beautiful Godchildren that we love and spoil dearly and a fantastic son that has been in my life since he was two months old. I'm not his biological father, but God granted me the blessing of being a part of his life since 2001.

Through it all, God has brought us through many trials of life, but nothing prepared us for the year of our Lord, 2020. (Please hear the sarcasm in my words) 2020 is a year that people across the planet will never forget. The coronavirus took the entire world by storm and changed the way of life as we once knew it to something that we never expected. I never thought I would see something like this change the spectrums of every nation. However, our pandemic experience differed because our year consisted of hospital entries, trips to the ER, multiple doctor visits, mental battles, anxiety attacks, addictions, and suicidal thoughts. So let's talk about it. The first five chapters of this book will cover my testimony of battling Diverticulitis and the mental and physical battles that came with it. I will share what God taught me in between the testimony through these battles. The last three chapters of this book will shed light on the importance of dealing with mental health and provide strategies to help you fight for your life and mind. I want to remind you that you are okay. You are not alone, and you don't have to fight alone. You're tough, but you're still human.

CHAPTER I
Life Interruptions — "Things To Come"

Romans 8:38-39

*For I am sure that neither death nor life, nor angels nor rulers, nor things present **nor things to come**, nor powers, nor height nor depth, nor anything else in all creation, will be able to separate us from the love of God in Christ Jesus our Lord. (Emphasis Added).*

In this scripture, Paul lists a few things that he refuses to allow to get between him and God. Out of all of the things he describes here, he speaks of one that truly stands out to me: "Nor things to come." This is a bold statement because Paul states, "I don't know what's going to come, and I don't know how hard it's going to come. But whatever comes, I will not allow it to get between my God and me." "Whatever Comes" is what I like to call interruptions. I am a die-hard Miami Hurricanes fan, and I remember one year while playing "FSWho, (Florida State for those that don't know)," there came an interruption during the game. I COULDN'T CARE LESS WHAT WAS HAPPENING! (It was a weather alert, but at that moment, I didn't care) Before the interruption came, an alert said, "We're sorry to disrupt your program, but this is a weather update for your local area." Again, I didn't care, we were about to score, and here I am looking at this! Ughhh! Luckily, I had my phone and watched it there. (Please don't follow my lead on that! I was dumb!) Just like the interruption during the game, interruptions in life always come at moments of inconvenience. They always break the flow of life. They never come at perfect moments; most people won't anticipate them. You planned to drive to your vacation destination with your family with the top down, music playing, and everything is going smooth.

> *Interruptions in life always come at moments of inconvenience.*

Suddenly, you have a blowout with no spare tire, and you're in the middle of nowhere.

You now miss your already paid-for flight, and there's no refund. On top of your blown-out tire, you look to find that your child's diaper blew out too! Ugh! You didn't plan to have a flat tire, a blowout diaper, and no spare tire. However, what if we had those disclaimers in life as on television? "I'm sorry to interrupt your life, but today, you will experience A, B, and C." Oh, how life could be so much easier. You could have been prepared for the blowout tire.

You would have checked under the car for the spare. You wouldn't have given your baby any extra food. Although we wouldn't like any of the above happenings, we could have at least prepared for them. Unfortunately, life doesn't give us an announcement before an interruption. It just happens, and that happened to me on February 11th, 2020.

The Interruption Begins

It was a cool brisk night, and the moon was shining bright. It was as if you could see every star in the sky. After an extraordinary meeting with our newly elected ministers and prophets, my wife and I were leaving our church. We had just spoken about our ministry's future endeavors, and I remember my wife grabbing my hand and saying, "I am excited to see what God is about to do at Life Changers." We were full of excitement as we went to grab something to eat and drove home talking about ministry. That night after eating, I felt pain in my lower abdomen that I had never felt before. Like everything else, I prayed that it would go away and just went to bed. However, I woke up at three in the morning, vomiting and in excruciating pain. I crawled back to my bed and lay in a fetal position, wondering what was happening. Again, I just prayed that whatever this was would run its course and pass on through. I finally dozed off and woke up a few hours later, only to find that the pain was still there. My life had been interrupted. I had about three meetings that day that I had to cancel. I stayed home and laid in bed all day which I hate doing. Around two that evening, the pain was still there, and so my wife, like most amazing wives have to do, told me to go to the E.R. I didn't think I needed to go but to keep the peace in my home, I went. Arriving at the E.R., my pain had eased up, and I thought this was a waste of time, but the lioness in my wife's voice said otherwise. After sitting in the waiting room and watching all the sick people coming in and out, I just sat in, still believing nothing was wrong with me. I started praying for everyone who went through the E.R. or those who sat next to me because I didn't think anything was wrong. Finally, they called my name, and my wife arrived to return with me. We walked back together and went through all of the protocols. After the exams, the staff wheeled me back to my room. My wife and I began to discuss the great meeting we had the night before with our newly elected ministers and prophets. We were so excited about what God was about to do. During that conversation, a nurse walks in and tells me, "We found something within your intestines. You have diverticulitis." Not knowing anything about it, my response was, "Okay, what do I need to do so that I can go home?" The nurse replied, "Well, we want to keep you here and give you antibiotics through I.V. in hopes that this will heal your intestines and we can get you better." Well, I didn't see that coming. I went in on a Thursday, planning everything I would do once I got out of here. I'm going to do A, B, and C, and then my wife and I will enjoy a Saturday evening of just chilling. However, none of that went as I planned it.

Once admitted, they started me on the I.V. medication. My pain was still there, but it seemed to shift a bit. Again, I didn't care. I had things to do. However, my body didn't do well with all the medication I received, and I started feeling extreme nausea. Because of this, they ordered me some nausea medicine to combat my feelings of nausea. The nurse came in, reached down, and grabbed my I.V. tube, and as soon as she put the treatment in my body, I began hallucinating. I had a horrible mental reaction to the medicine. Immediately as the drugs went in, I slowly lost my mind. I tried to pray in my head but couldn't even focus. Nothing made sense, and I became terrified because I had never felt this way. I had no control over my mind. I had compressors around my legs to prevent blood clots, and I thought they were snakes. I tore them off in complete fear. I almost pulled the I.V. out of my arm because I thought it was a snake trying to bite me. I began to rock back and forth uncontrollably. I couldn't catch my breath, and my wife had to hold on to me with all her might to console me. She had to walk me into what seemed like a long deserted hallway. The hallway almost resembled one of those hallways you see in those Jason/Freddy Krueger movies. We walked the halls for about 30 minutes. I trembled in fear because I had no earthly idea what was happening. I didn't know that I was reacting to the medication. All I could do was cry and pray. We finally returned to the room, and I lay in the bed weeping. I put a worship song on by Todd Dulaney, and I had to sing myself to sleep.

Waking up the next day, I was no better. My mood had changed, I was tired and trembling, and I felt like a zombie. I remember praying to God and asking, "What's going on?" I wish I had a powerful statement to write about what was said, but it was nothing. I couldn't preach that Sunday, as I was hoping to do, because I was still in the hospital. However, I honestly had no desire to preach. I had no desire for anything at that moment. My whole mind and mood had been altered. I thank God for Elder Turner, one of the leaders of our church, who stepped up and carried the service for me. That evening I lay in that hospital bed, fighting with all my might to keep my sanity. The next day I was released to go home and begin taking the medication given through the I.V. by mouth. Nothing got better. On top of the initial pain, I have a mental battle I've never experienced. My wife got me home, and I just laid down on our couch and cried. My living room had begun to feel like a prison. The Peace of God that once felt easy to tap into somehow disappeared. Sometimes in the moments of pain and suffering, it feels like God's presence is far from you. However, those thoughts aren't true, but in those moments, what's a lie begins to feel like a reality. My wife was holding me, and she even felt distant from me. When you're scared or in a moment of uncertainty, it's hard to feel anything. It's not that God or your loved ones aren't close by; it's because what you think is what you become and nothing more. At that moment, I felt crazy, and nothing else could change that. But I praise God for a God that doesn't leave us based on our feelings, and I thank God for a strong woman of God that didn't leave my side either. Two weeks went by, and nothing changed but the medication. For two weeks, my wife would just come and pray over me, but at that moment, I couldn't do anything but cry and remember all the things we had just planned. I just knew for sure that this was going to get better. Unfortunately, it didn't. I got a call to go into the doctor's office, and that's when my life was indeed interrupted. "Mr. Valentine, we'll have to perform surgery on you ASAP! We're going to remove and reconstruct your intestine" Wait! What?

Two weeks ago, I was planning to pour into the minsters; two weeks later, I'm standing in front of a stranger I now have to trust with my life. On top of that, I didn't wake up thinking I needed a reserve amount of money in my bank account to pay for a surgery that I didn't know I needed. Don't get me wrong, we save money, and we have good insurance, but we just had to pay for tires on both our cars, major repairs on our home from a storm that had just passed through, and my son was just hit by a drunk driver and lost one of his eyes, and we were taking care of him. But interruptions don't care. That's why they're called INTERRUPTIONS. Interruptions don't care if you're behind on your bills or have a loved one in need. Interruptions don't care that you're a preacher with a ton of faith. It's going to come. Interruptions are like playing hide and go seek, and it's the seeker, and it says, "Ready or not, here I come!" And you're in the BEST hiding place in God, and it still finds you. Trouble finding you does not mean that you're not in the Secret Place (The Presence of God). Trouble finds the best of us. So, I had to meet with my church and my family and let them know what would happen. I remember driving home with a million questions running through my mind. Due to my cancer ten years ago,

I had to have portions of my colon and intestine removed. There was a huge possibility of having to have a colostomy bag if I ever had intestinal surgery again. Not again, I thought. Why me? Why NOW! God, I have to preach! I have couples that I'm counseling! I have a conference to prepare for! I need to be here for my wife! I have ministers that I have to prepare! Again, Interruptions don't care.

Interruptions can make you experience two types of feelings: Uncertainty and Insecurity. Interruptions make us feel uncomfortable because we have no control over the moment. All we can do is trust, pray, cry, and wait. You can manage a planned day, but only God can control an interrupted day. Interruptions interrupt our faith, our worship, our praise, our joy, and our stability. We believe strongly in what we are singing about until an interruption comes and causes us to question and look again at what we believe. Interruptions allow you to know that you don't have as much control of your life as you thought. We need only look to the coronavirus pandemic as an example of how quickly life could change. None of us would have imagined turning our bedrooms into a work office or changing our dining rooms into a classroom for our children. Let alone losing the joy of personal contact with family. We must ask this question to ourselves about life interruptions; in whose hands do I put this? In the hands of God, interruptions can work for us. In the hands of the enemy, interruptions can work against us. God uses interruptions to either get our attention, change our hearts/lives, adjust our focus, draw us closer, or simply show Himself to us in a different way. The enemy does the complete opposite. He will use it to make us angry towards

> *Only God can control an interrupted day*

God, stop walking in our purpose, harden our hearts toward people, and make us bitter towards God. Although I don't like interruptions, I'm grateful that my interruptions are in the hands of the Lord. That doesn't mean I didn't cry, feel pain (as you will read a little later), or become distraught. It means I found a pillow in the lion's den, shelter in the storm, and rest in the prison of the moment. And I believe you will too.

We must understand that "Things to come" will come, but I pray that you make the declaration as Paul did, "It won't separate me from the love of Christ Jesus." We don't know what tomorrow may bring, but we know who will be in our tomorrow. I have had to learn that nothing surprises God. We are surprised but not God. God is not just in our tomorrow, but He's already at the end. I think of a marathon race and all the people standing on the sidelines rooting for the runners as they run. They also have stations for the runners to grab water as they run. God is all that for us, and He is at the beginning of the race. He's with us while we're running the race. The Lord is also the stand on the side, providing you water and waiting on you to celebrate at the finish line. God is in our beginning, middle, and end. Just because our Father is with us doesn't mean we don't get tired or flustered. However, it does mean that God is there regardless of what we're going through. And He is a support on which we can lean. He's also in your tomorrow while encouraging you to run on today.

"The major problem of life is learning how to handle the costly interruptions. The door that slams shut, the plan that got sidetracked, the marriage that failed. Or that lovely poem that didn't get written because someone knocked on the door."

Martin Luther King Jr.

CHAPTER II
Get Up!

Psalms 28:7

The Lord is my strength and my shield; in him my heart trusts, and I am helped; my heart exults, and with my song I give thanks to him.

On the eve of my surgery, I woke up full of optimism and faith that morning. It was a beautiful sunny Sunday morning. The sun was shining ever so brightly, and I just knew that today would be a good day. My usual routine on Sunday mornings on my way to church is to call and hear my parents' voices and check on them. This particular morning I didn't get an answer. Again, full of optimism and faith, I just figured they were getting ready for church themselves and didn't have any time to talk. So I went on my way, blasting my worship music, hand out the window gliding through the wind with my bride by my side. The morning couldn't have been any better. We got to church, and WE HAD CHURCH! God's presence was so heavy in that place, and it was every bit of what I needed. I shared with my congregation that everything was going to be okay. We prayed, shouted, cried, and shouted some more. Aww, man, there's nothing like a RIGHT NOW PRAISE.

After everyone left, my wife and I just sat in there for a few moments, and with smiles on our faces, we said everything was going to be okay. Just like the night we left from our meeting mentioned in the opener of this book, we left the same way from service. The only difference was that the sun was bright instead of the moon. We could have skipped to the car because that's how jubilant we felt. That all changed once I looked at my phone and saw that I had a voicemail from my sister. I listened to the voicemail, and my heart just dropped. After an amazing service that was a God-filled encounter, here comes an interruption. My sister informed me that my father was rushed to the ER that morning because he was unresponsive and didn't know what was happening. This situation was why they didn't answer the phone. I didn't understand. How could we have a service like the one we just had, and while I'm praising God for how good He is, my father is fighting for his life in the E.R.? These were the thoughts rushing through my head. Life doesn't stop because we're praising God. However, we shouldn't allow life to change our mindset on the God we serve. We rushed to the hospital and walked in on my father, lying on the table, on a breathing machine with tubes coming out of his body. He couldn't talk, nor could he respond. All he could do was look up towards the ceiling. At that moment, I felt myself becoming angry and confused. My mother sat down and began praying, and all we could do at that moment was trust God. All I could do was think about the service we had just had and now this. I was getting encouraging messages from members about the service, but they had no idea that I was reading them from my father's hospital room. I had become so hurt because I had never seen my father like this. While sitting there, I told my family that I would not have the surgery. I can't be in the hospital, and my father is like this. I'm not going to have the surgery. My mother and my wife talked me into going through with my procedure the next day. With anger and pain in my heart, I succumbed and went home to prepare for the next day.

My cousins Thandi and Jerome and my dear brother Pastor Derrick Morrisette came over and sat with us that evening, and God knew what we needed. People to cry with, smile with, and weep with some more.

> *God sends distractions to take our eyes off of our problems.*

Some distractions come and try and make you take your eyes off God, and then there are those distractions that God sends to get us to take our eyes off our problems. They were our distractions from God. For those next few hours, it was a moment of peace. The next day came, and all of the praise and joy I had the day before was gone. I couldn't sleep at all that night because my mind was still on my father, mom, and health. It's easy to smile, but it's also hard to forget the current battle that you're facing at the moment. My mind had a field day that night. The one million and one questions that flowed through my head didn't allow me to sleep at all. We got up the next day to head to the hospital. My mother had told me that my father had improved, which brought some peace to me. Arriving at the ER, my Spiritual Parents, Apostle Andra and Cynthia Cunningham, greeted us. Man, they were a blessing and a relief to see. God always blesses us with people to walk with us through the fires and trials of life. They truly helped carry our burdens (Galatians 6:2). The time finally came for me to go back for the procedure. I remember kissing my wife on the hand and she telling me that everything was going to be alright. Being wheeled back to the O.R., I remembered having to battle my mind about all of the what-ifs that could take place. The only thing I could think to do was sing the song, "Precious Lord, take my hand, lead me on, let me stand." I sang that song so loud that they cut the music down in the O.R. I sang it so that when they put me to sleep, I could still hear it in my mind. I remembered growing up listening to the saints of old sing that song. There were times I would hear my Grandmother hum it while cooking, and it just felt right to me at that moment. That song carried me through this whole journey. The surgery was scheduled to be an hour and thirty minutes but lasted four and a half hours. The doctor told my wife that it was a tough surgery. They ran across places within me that didn't show up on the CT, and they found a mass the size of a grown man's fists put together. It never showed up on the CT. I never felt it until a few weeks ago, and even then, it wasn't that noticeable. My wife has the pictures of that mass, but up until this day, I haven't looked at it.

Waking up to my wife's face was the best feeling in the world. However, the pain I felt from the surgery was extremely agonizing. I had tubes coming out of everywhere, and I was confused and wanted to know what was happening. My wife explained everything that the doctor told her and the last statement he made was, "he should be good now." Okay. I should be good now. That was all I needed to hear. One thing I will say, you want to talk about interruptions, try sleeping in a hospital. Once you become comfortable, they interrupt you to check your vitals, bathe you at 3 am, give meds, etc. No rest! The next day, I was lying in the hospital bed, and the PT Nurse walked in. In my mind, I'm wondering, what are you doing here? Of course, I knew what her job was, but still. It's the next day. Surely I'm not going to have to do anything the next day. She then walks up to my bed and begins to ask me questions about my procedure, and she then tells me that she's here to do some Physical Therapy with me. I was cool with it because I thought it would just back exercise. Nope. She said all I'm going to ask you to do is, get up. Of course, I told her, "Ma'am, I just had major surgery, and you want me to get up?" Her reply with a face full of excitement was, "Yep." I told her that I couldn't do it, and she said that I could. In my mind, I didn't believe that I could move, but after about 20-25 minutes of grunting, crying, and pain, I got up. The pillow you see me holding on the front page was the one I had to use when I got up.

I didn't realize that what I faced within those 20-25 minutes was a foreshadowing of the following months. It's going to be hard, but get up. You probably don't want to, but get up! You're going to have tears in your eyes, but GET UP! Don't let your mind tell you that you can't do what your heart is pushing you to do; GET UP! I couldn't stand that nurse, but she pushed me. She knew how to position me not to hurt myself as I got up. God knows, although we're in pain, He knows how to position us and coach us on how to angle our bodies so that we don't hurt ourselves as we're struggling to get up. In Psalms 28:7 (a), David says, "The Lord is my strength and my shield; in him my heart trusts, and I am helped." He is our strength to get up. Some shields were so big that they were used for protection and as a support for the Soldier as he got back up from kneeling. God is our shield of protection and our shield of support, and in Him, my heart trusts. David then goes on to say, "And I am HELPED." You're not going to receive help; you already have help. You are receiving help right now. God offers His support to help you, GET UP! The shield of faith isn't there only to protect you but to support you. This situation will not defeat you my friend!

> *The shield of faith isn't there only to protect you but to support you.*

There is another chapter to your story, GET UP! Take a moment and say, "I have more chapters to my life, and this will not defeat me!" It may change you, but it won't defeat you. I was in pain sitting on the edge of that bed, but I was up. I learned how to look beyond the pain while seeing the small victories. Getting up was hard, but the reward of getting up is the determination for the next move within life. Winners don't always look like winners. A wounded warrior is still a warrior. I remember years ago, after watching a Super Bowl game, one of the players from the winning team came to the podium with his arm in a sling, a bandage around his ribs, and cuts and bruises. However, it didn't matter how he looked; he was still a winner. He was a champion. And guess what, you may not look like it, you may not feel like it, but you are a champion. You're standing behind the podium of life with bruises, pain, a broken heart, a challenged spirit, but you're still a champion. Life doesn't dictate who and what you are. You are a champion!

When I got up when the nurse asked, it seemed like my determination and drive woke up. The next few days, I started sitting up in the bed for a few moments at a time. I told my wife that I wanted to walk around the room. I didn't need that nurse anymore. All she had to do was wake up the champion in me, and my Helper did the rest. My father was in the hospital right along with me, and I hadn't had a chance to see him. My mother was going back and forth to our rooms. With my now drive, I made up in my mind that I would see my father. I got a walker and walked to the elevator with my wife and the Holy Ghost to the fourth floor to see my father. It hurt, but I made it. What a blessing it was to see my father. He was now responsive, talking, and up. We cried and praised God for that moment. Some of you may say that I was doing too much, but I knew that's what I was supposed to do. Walk as much as you can. Believe me, I was drugged up most of the time and I would sleep about 3/4 of the day and walk when I could, but I had to see my father that day. Now that I began to gain a little of my strength back, I was starting to revisit the plans that we had made for our ministry. I was getting excited because I could see what I thought was the light at the end of the tunnel. However, my body wasn't taking too well to the surgery. I was supposed to be in the hospital for only a week, but I was still there after eight days. They were waiting on my body to begin functioning again, but it wasn't. I was still in extreme pain. I was supposed to be getting ready for discharge the next day; however, I am now preparing for another CT lab scan. I came back to the room later that evening, around 3 o'clock. My wife was in the room praying and she just held my hand as we waited to see what was going on. The doctor and a few of his colleagues came in behind him, and they all had a certain look on their faces. I knew something wasn't right. With no hesitation, they told me that I had become septic. My kidneys were failing, and my intestines had opened up - the surgery didn't take. They informed me that I would have to have a colostomy bag and wound vac. Before this entire surgery, I purposely prayed to God not to have a colostomy bag. I knew that this was a possibility because of my bout with cancer, but again I prayed and I believed that this wouldn't happen. And guess what, it did. I asked the doctor when this surgery would be, and they said, "NOW! You have no time to waste." They gave us a few moments to gather ourselves together and pray. Again, an interruption doesn't prepare you for what's to come, nor does it forewarn you that it's coming. Here I am preparing to go home and get back to God's work, and nope. Not Yet! My wife and mother are the strongest women I know. My wife and mother are soldiers. They don't cry much. They're both strong warriors for the Lord, but to see them cry was one of the most challenging moments. I was afraid, and seeing my wife's face full of fear and uncertainty was harder than the surgery itself. As they wheeled me down the hall, I could hear her crying from the room. My heart sunk to a place of hopelessness, confusion, and simply numbness. I could still hear the cries of my wife and mother. But as I was lying on that bed, looking back up at the all too familiar lights, I heard someone praying. It was my transporter. Her name was Sheril Lynn. We grew up together. She had tears in her eyes, but she was praying. I truly believe she was an angel from God. Many people will talk about the story of Jesus in Matthew 4 on how He defeated the enemy successfully with the Word of God, but I hardly ever hear anyone talk about is this part:

Matthew 4:11- Then the devil leaveth him, and, behold, angels came and ministered unto him.

The Angels came and ministered to Jesus. If Jesus needed to receive ministry, who are we not to need the same thing. There will be a point in your life where life will happen, and you're going to need ministry. Not preaching but ministry; the two are entirely different. (Side note: some people need to learn the difference. I don't need a sermon; I need a shoulder) That woman of God prayed for me all the way down there, and I found myself singing again, "Precious Lord, Take My Hand" while she was praying. As they laid me on the table to perform surgery, I could hear the voice of my PT nurse saying, "Get Up!" She wasn't talking to my physical man but my soul. Although I had prayed and sang, my soul became low. David had this to happen to him, and he asked his soul a question:

Psalms 43:5 – Why are you downcast, O my soul? Why the unease within me? Put your hope in God, for I will yet praise Him, my Savior and my God.

I had to tell my soul, "Get UP!" I had to encourage myself while falling asleep. You will not die! You will rise again! Get UP! I had to tell my soul, get up! Some of the nurses in the room heard me humming, and they had begun to pray with me. I had to put my hope back in God and to my expectations. I had to put my Hope in His will and His understanding. We sometimes have to redirect our thoughts and our hope and place them back on and in God and not on what we think or wish to happen. And that, my friend, is not always easy.

"If life knocks you down, try to land on your back. Because if you can look up, you can get up. And if you get up, you can stand up. And if you stand up, you can fight for your dream once again. You have something special. You have GREATNESS within you!"

Les Brown

CHAPTER III
Yet, I Am Not Alone

John 16:32

Look, an hour is coming and has already come when you will be scattered, each to his own home, and you will leave Me all alone. Yet I am not alone because the Father is with Me.

Jesus makes a statement that holds so true within our lives. He knew that a time was drawing near that the people who walked with Him for miles would no longer walk with Him. However, Jesus knew that they would leave Him, but HE also knows of someone that won't, and that's God. I am alone physically, but I'm not alone spiritually because the Father is with Me. "The Father is with me" is a daily statement we must remind ourselves of. God is with me. It's easier said than done because although we know that God is with us, we long for the touch of our loved ones or the shoulder of our best friend. Unfortunately, sometimes, they won't be there. They won't answer the call. Not because they're rejecting you, but maybe the phone was on silent, or they were asleep. Whatever the case, when you needed them, they weren't there. Jesus also understood this, which is why He sent us the Holy Spirit. In Greek, the Holy Spirit is known as the: Parakletos (par- rah-clay-tus), "the one who comes alongside." The Holy Spirit has always shown up in critical moments, such as being abandoned, alone, or in places of discomfort. He was with the three Hebrew boys in the fire, Daniel in the Lion's Den, David in his moments of despair and depression, Paul and Silas in prison, etc. You see,

God's presence doesn't eliminate us from the problem, but it does give us protection and strength within the problem. All the places I mentioned that God was present were not places of comfort but trouble. God is with you. He walks alongside you. In Psalms 23:4(b), David said, "I will fear no evil because You are WITH ME." Sometimes in life, when interrupted, we tend to lose focus on this very thing. What we feel may not be accurate. You may feel alone, but you are not alone!

After returning from my emergency surgery, I awakened to a room full of nurses surrounding me, poking, probing, and talking to me. I saw my father at my bedside, my mother with tears in her eyes, and my wife with a smile that was not doing a good job covering up the pain in her eyes. I then tried to grab my wife's hand and felt an object connected to me. I looked down, and I saw this bag hanging from my stomach. Then I saw all of this tape on my stomach. I then remembered that I was to get a colostomy bag. My wife had to explain everything because I knew nothing about a Colostomy Bag or a Wound Vac. I lay there in disbelief because, again, the very thing I didn't want was the same thing I now have. (I realized later that what I didn't want to have saved my life) After coming to grips with my reality, I remember feeling more pain. They gave me a pump with a mixture of pain medication and, every two hours, a shot of Dilaudid. I had terrible veins, so they had to run a pic line on the upper part of my arm to get all of the medicine I needed in my body. I just wanted to sleep in hopes that everything would go away. It only got worse. We often want to wish our problems away, but they are not going away. I had to learn how to deal with it. Not in

> *I just wanted to sleep in hopes that everything would go away.*

the sense of saying to get over it like it isn't a big deal, but I had to learn how to deal with my current situation.

The Coronavirus Pandemic had just begun to hit our state of Alabama, and the hospital was now beginning to shut down. The next day my mother had just walked into my room and sat down when one of my nurses came and told her, "Ma'am, I am sorry, you have to leave. We're only allowing one visitor per patient." My mom returned to my father. My wife and I were wondering, 'what in the world was going on?' Because we were in the hospital, we had no clue what was happening outside the hospital's four walls. This situation angered me because I knew my mother and wife were good for helping each other through this situation, but what could I do? A new PT nurse came in after my mother left and asked, "Do you think you can get up for me?" I looked at him sideways. If I could have Karate Judo

Chopped him, I would have. But I remembered the importance of getting up. This time I had tubes and a bag hanging from me. I remember what my old PT taught me, but it wasn't working. I had to learn a new way of getting up. Sometimes in life, we have to readjust our way of getting up. We can master one way, but now you have new attachments causing you to adjust. But you can, and you will get up. I sat up in my bed full of pain and cried while holding my wife and telling her thank you for being there for me. My PT nurse was so amazing and encouraging. He hyped me up so much that I stood up to walk but quickly realized NOPE! I thought it best to chill out. After a pretty challenging day, night came. A nurse walks in and tells my wife that she has to leave in the midst of me resting. Due to the Pandemic, we must remove all visitors from the premises. WHAT? NO! I was too weak to say anything. However, I told them, you can't make her go home. She has to stay with me. They eventually allowed her to stay the night; I'm so glad she did. They allowed her to go home, get clothes, and return to the hospital with me. When my wife returned, I was too doped up and weak to realize that she had returned. But I remember hearing her having a strong conversation with one of the nurses that quickly opened my eyes. Because of the pandemic, they had to switch around nurses who wouldn't usually work with patients like me. I ended up having a nurse that worked in the children's area.

I was becoming so weak because my kidneys had begun to fail. My body, again, was not responding well to the surgery. Thank God for my wife. She saw that all of my vital signs were beginning to drop and called every nurse in there. I don't know what she said or did, but I had doctors and nurses at my bedside before I knew it. All I could do was just lay there and thank God for an Angel being by my side. When morning came, one of my nurses said that the Governor had deemed this a state of emergency, and everyone had to leave. We tried everything to get my wife to stay, but nothing worked. She had to pack up her bags and leave, and there I was, alone. We both were. My wife was my rock. She was my anchor. What am I going to do now? The moment my wife left was when I felt all of my desire and strength leave. I was angry! Mad! Frustrated! Alone! I cried for hours because I felt abandoned. I became extremely sick to the point that I couldn't hold anything down, and they had to give me an NG Tube. I didn't know what was happening and became irritated with life. I didn't want to watch TV. I didn't want to do anything but look out the window. That's when I started noticing birds. (We'll talk about this a little later) Out of the blue, I get a phone call from my Spiritual Grandfather, Apostle Maurice K. Wright. When I saw his name on my phone, I lit up. I answered the phone, and he just spoke a few simple words to me, "Grandson, you're going to be okay. God is with you." He couldn't talk long because he was battling a sickness, which none of us knew. He called at one of the lowest points of my life, and God knew I needed to hear those words. To hear his voice was a blessing to me, and God strengthened me through him. Those few words carried me through a plethora of tough times. One, in particular, was a time when I had PT, and It wasn't a good day to start with that activity. After completing the therapy, I got back in the bed, and my nurse, not intentionally, set my phone and call button far from my bed, and I couldn't get anything for the pain. I lay there for almost an hour, alone, crying and singing, until the cleaning lady walked in and rushed to get some help. (I don't fault the nurses because this was during the beginning of the pandemic, and they were scattered all over the building) But God was with me. I found myself battling within my mind. My body was so weak, and I began losing a lot of weight and hope. At this point, almost a month has gone by, and I'm still here.

Sunsets had lost their beauty with me. Whenever I saw the sunset, no matter how beautiful it was, it reminded me that nighttime was coming. Nights were the hardest. Due to the pandemic, they had to move us into certain hospital areas because the rooms were overcrowded with patients. In doing this, I was placed next to psych ward patients, and one of them just screamed all night long. (He was the reason the nurses couldn't hear me when I was crying for help. Every time I asked for help, he would scream over me) However, I remembered the words of my spiritual grandmother. God is with you. I then begin to pray and sing. I told God, I don't know what you're doing, but I know I'm in your hands. I know that you will make a way. All I want to do is see my wife. I don't want to hear her voice. I don't want to see her through video. I want her to be right here next to me. And God heard me. Because of the wound vac, they found a way to bring my wife back to change my bandages. They thought they would teach her, but that woman already knew what to do. She was a PRO! She could only come for about 20 minutes a day, but those were the best 20 minutes of my life. God showed me that He not only hears the words that we say but the tears that we cry. God knows what He's doing because the very thing I hated having was the thing He used to get her up there. Some things God allows to come into your life don't make sense at the moment, but they are blessings and tools for God to work wonders. God allowed the bag attachment for two reasons: first, to save my life, and second because He knew the pandemic would happen. He knew that my wife was going to have to leave me. However, He knew the policy to get her back up there. None of this made sense to me at that moment, but it made perfect sense afterward. Back to feeling alone. While in the hospital rooms, I began to understand what Jesus said in the above Scripture, "Yet, I am not alone because the Father is with me." I had faced many trials and moments of loneliness until this point, but nothing like this. Side note: if you don't know what a Colostomy bag is, it's simply a bag for waste. There was a time when my bag had busted in my bed, and I was pretty embarrassed and frustrated. My focus had shifted to everything going wrong, the life adjustments, and just feeling

> *Yet, I am not alone because the Father is with me.*

hopeless. The nurse came in and reminded me that it was okay. The janitor came in a reminded me that it was okay. My wife had to call and remind me that it was okay. But I didn't feel okay. Then a scripture came across my phone, Isaiah 41:10-"Don't be afraid, because I'm with you; don't be anxious, because I am your God. I keep on strengthening you; I'm truly helping you. I'm surely upholding you with my victorious right hand." The Holy Spirit had to remind me; that I keep strengthening you! From day to day, I keep strengthening you. God doesn't stop pouring His mercy, love, strength, and drive into us.

He keeps on pouring. Regardless of the circumstance, God keeps pouring out His strength. The more life throws at you; the more God keeps on strengthening you. This is why He's our daily bread. He's our daily strength. God gives us daily strength because there are daily battles that we face.

God pours out His strength to us through others. I wish I could say that God spoke to me through an open majestic heaven that manifested above me, angels filled my room, and I felt God's Glory. Although I did feel God's presence, everything else was just a thought. However, God did strengthen me through the nurses, one in particular. I'm 6'8", three hundred and … sumthin pounds (that's none of ya business), and this little old fireball lady comes in there and wrecks my whole day. (In a good way) After having the night I had before, the Lord knew what I needed. This woman got me out of that bed; boy, she was something else. She would grab me and say, pointing her little old finger at me, "Now, man of God, you have work to do! You will not stay down!" Over three weeks, I found myself smiling more and pressing forth because of this little ole lady. God began to distract me again and shift my focus on Him, not the situation. The conversations between my wife and me were more about the experiences we had with God and less about our situation. Not to say that it wasn't hard, but our focus was shifting. Although we were alone, God was definitely with us. I begin to look at the moments of being in the hospital as moments of God wanting to spend time with me. Although I would have been better off spending time with Him at home, I get it. The revelations I received from God in that hospital couldn't have come to me elsewhere. God had to show me that He is my provider. As much as I love my wife, He was my rock. Through the moments of frustration, God comforted my heart and didn't allow my mind to go crazy. God spoke to me through some of the nurses, the cleaning lady, the birds outside my window (Again, we will talk about this later), and the silent moments. I thought I knew God until I had to trust Him. I sang songs of worship that I'd never heard before. I began to pray in a way that I'd never prayed before. I began to experience God's presence like I never had before. I was still hurting, still having my moments of crying, but I began to embrace this new level of worship. I had become open and honest to God, and He became the same with me. You honestly can't fake it with God when it's just you and Him. He never promised any of us a life of splendor and blessings. The old hymn goes, "Nobody told me that the road would be easy, but I don't believe, He's brought me this far to leave me." And God hasn't. Christ spoke more about suffering than He did blessings. He told us we could have houses, lands, blessings, and persecutions (Mark 10:29-30). He never left out the reality of life. He never promised us a bed of roses on earth. He did, however, promise us that no matter what happens, no matter who comes or who goes, He would always be there. He never promised us a life outside the fire, but He promised He would be in the fire. Some of us can't see God for who He is until we enter the fire. The manifested presence of God may not show up outside the fire but in it. Again, we don't like it, but there's something to be found within this fire. That is why the Devil is fighting you so hard. You won't see God within if he can get you to focus on the fire. There's a side of God that will manifest in your storm right now. It will all make perfect sense soon.

A story that truly blessed me in the Bible was when David came back from war to Ziklag and found that the Amalekites had wrecked it and all of their children and wives had been kidnapped. (I will go more in-depth on this story a little later) The Bible says that the men wept bitterly, so much so that they had no more tears to cry. They then turned on David out of frustration. David then goes by himself and cries all the more. He then encourages himself in the Lord, asks for the Ephod for prayer, and goes before the Lord. What I love about this story is not what David did but God's response. God didn't get mad at David, nor did He rebuke David. He allowed David the opportunity to cry and vent. When we're alone with the Lord, God doesn't restrict us from crying and expressing our true feelings. When you need to cry, cry. When you need to scream, scream. You may need to have a "Here, hit Weazer" moment from Steel Magnolias movie (If you haven't seen that movie, shame on you), punch a pillow. Whatever you do, do it, but don't forget that God is with you, and He doesn't restrict you from expressing your emotions. But after you've gotten it all out, go before the Lord and let Him pour back into you. He loves you more than you will ever know. God taught me this during my first month in the hospital. Cry, be angry, but know that God still loves you, and He's still with you. Isaiah 43:2 (ESV) - When you pass through the waters, I will be with you; and through the rivers, they shall not overwhelm you; when you walk through fire you shall not be burned, and the flame shall not consume you.

"You are never left alone when you are alone with God."

Woodrow Kroll

CHAPTER IV
I Thought It Would Be Better By Now

1 Peter 4:12-13 (NLT)

Dear friends, don't be surprised at the fiery trials you are going through, as if something strange were happening to you. Instead, be very glad— for these trials make you partners with Christ in his suffering, so that you will have the wonderful joy of seeing his glory when it is revealed to all the world.

Many of us have faced trials and tribulations within our lifetime. Although we don't like them, the biggest issue we deal with within the tribulations of life is the length of the tribulation. How long will this last? When will it be over? When will I get back to normal? I thought I would be better by now! These are the thoughts that travel through all of our minds and mine as well. They traveled through my mind like the children of Israel wandering through the desert. I cried these questions. Unanswered questions can bring about many raw emotional feelings. We try to understand what's happening, but nothing brings a solution. Another issue that arises when we're dealing with our interruptions is our expectations to be over whatever we're dealing with at the moment. We want to be back to normal. We want to feel like it never happened. We want to escape our right-now reality. This is how I felt while transitioning home. My expectations for things going back to normal were extremely high because I was now returning home, and we all know that there's no place like home. It was a beautiful morning on the day of my release from the hospital. I was excited to go home finally. My surgery was on

March 10th, and I didn't get released from the hospital until around April 10th. I woke up that morning excited to be able to see my wife and my family. The nurses were so happy to see me leave, and as much as I had grown to like them, I was glad to no longer have to see them. As I began to gather myself together, I now had a bag attached to my body that I had to watch out for, as well as a womb vac bag that I had to carry on my shoulder and make sure not to step on the cord that now hangs from my stomach. That brought a little bit of hopelessness to my mind, but I'm going home. All the nurses lined up and down the hall and clapped as I was wheeled out to meet my wife. I had tears in my eyes because I thought I would die in that hospital. The older nurse I mentioned in the last chapter signed the pillow that I'm holding on the cover of this book, pointed her little finger at me, and said, "You gone on home and let the good Lord heal you up." As she wheeled me outside, I was greeted by the most incredible smile God had ever created. My wife came up and hugged me so gently, but it somehow felt like she just squeezed life into me. She somehow lifted me into the car, and we drove off, and I remembered looking out the hospital window with tears flowing from my eyes. My mother in-love and little nephew had come down to help take some pressure off my wife while she was at home alone. I walked into my house and was greeted with love; all I could do was just thank God. I lifted my hands and just began to praise God for His goodness. I told my wife that I wanted to go somewhere, but she had to remind me that we were in a pandemic and everything was closed. I was a bit confused because while in the hospital, I didn't watch the news that much and wasn't fully aware of all that was happening in the world. I had enough problems of my own to worry about anything else.

However, I just sat in my chair and felt alive and thankful to be home. Unfortunately, all of that excitement slowly begin to drift away. I didn't expect the next phase of trials to come my way.

> *I didn't expect the next phase of trials to come my way.*

While in surgery, they put a strap over my leg that helped keep me secure on the table, but it was placed tightly over my leg, which pinched my Sciatic nerve. This caused my right leg to be in pain and become extremely hot. It was treated in the hospital but worsened once I returned home. I was given three different medications, on top of at least 20 different other pills I had to take. The pills I was given were for epileptic patients, but I was told they could help with nerve pain. Because I had just had this major surgery and my leg was on fire, I could not sleep in my bed, so I had to sleep in my recliner in my game room. (Yes, I have my own Miami

Hurricane Game Room/Man Cave) My wife was so awesome that she stayed back with me every night. A few days into being home, I slowly sank into a place I'd never been before: depression, hopelessness, frustration, and anger. My wife had to change my Colostomy bag because I couldn't come to grips with looking at it. It took me around a month to clean it on my own because I couldn't process what was happening mentally. One particular evening I began to feel pain in my stomach that reminded me of the pain I had felt that sent me to the hospital, and I started to panic because I thought something else was wrong. Again, God hears our tears because although I never said anything, I had an uncle, a good friend, and a deacon from our old church to call me and coach me through the ups and downs. These men had endured what I was going through and began to help guide me to a place of understanding. Before I spoke with them, I honestly felt alone. I felt like no one understood my situation. This is a lie that the enemy will place in your mind to make you feel isolated from God and your brothers and sisters. This is why your testimony is so important. It's liberating for others to hear your story of how you made it over. These men were a blessing because no one warns you of recovery at home. I wasn't warned about the complications of the colostomy bag. We weren't warned about the ups and downs of body temperature changes. No one told me that my serotonin levels would be off. Serotonin helps with your happy mood and mood swings; it's created within your stomach. When you have a major surgery within your abdomen, as I had, it alters your body's ability to produce serotonin to keep you joyful. The results of low serotonin can be depression, insomnia, low self-esteem, loss of appetite, and so much more. I experienced everything there was to experience in dealing with this. It frustrated me so much. I wanted to be happy, but I couldn't. I just sat and cried. I never lashed out at my wife, but I did lash out at myself as if I had anything to do with what was happening to me. Since I knew none of the information I just stated above, I honestly thought something was wrong with me. I wasn't sent home with anything to forewarn me of what would happen once I got home. And you know what? That's life! We don't have a blueprint for living life after a loved one has passed. There are no instructions on recuperating after a significant adjustment to your daily life. We all think adjustments are easy until it becomes you that's having to do the adjusting. I praise God for the men who opened up about their experiences. Although there's no blueprint for dealing with your situation, a pioneer has walked down the road you're currently on, and God has placed them in your life to strengthen, educate, and encourage you. I'm reminded of a story. It's been told many different ways, but I heard it from a preacher on television one day. It's the story of a man that fell into a hole. A guy was walking one day and ended up falling into a hole. The hole was very steep, and when he landed, he saw that he had broken his foot on the way down. The man noticed that the hole was too steep to escape and he was too hurt even to try. He sees a doctor who walks by the hole and shouts, "Hey doc, can you please help me out of this hole? I'm hurt, and I can't get out." The doctor reaches into his coat, pulls out a pad, and proceeds to write a prescription for the man. "Here, use this once you get out." He throws the prescription in the hole and walks off. He then sees a preacher walking by. "Hey, Rev, can you please help me out of this hole?" The preacher reaches into his pocket, pulls out a pen, and writes a few Bible verses on the paper. The preacher then threw the scriptures in the hole with the man. "Here, read these and pray while you're down there." The preacher then walks off. By this time, the man is becoming frustrated and tired. He sees someone walking by, and he looks grimly and says, "Sir, can you please help me? I don't need a - "Booom! The man heard a huge thud in the hole. And to his surprise, the man that was just above him is now in the hole with him. "You dummy, what are you doing? Now we're both stuck down here." The man looked at him and said, "Don't worry, I have been here before, and I know how to get out." Whew, the first time I heard that story, it blessed me tremendously. That story played out when those brothers came through and jumped in the hole of life with me and helped me navigate through the pain and frustration that was new to me but old to them. NOTE: The following paragraph contains graphic medical details; please skip to the next section if such information is difficult for you to read.

One of the most challenging parts of all of this was that my wound vac was extremely close to my colostomy bag and would cause many complications. Again, if you don't know what a colostomy bag is, it's a bag that handles your body's stool. Sometimes my colostomy bag would leak waste into the womb vac area, and my wife would have to clean it along with my womb vac area. What is a wound vac? A wound vac is placed over a deep wound on your body that helps keep that area from getting infected. My stomach was cut into two pieces, and I had about an 8-9 inch gap in my stomach. It was excruciating having to remove all of the tape from around my stomach, but my wife was an angel. She would wake up in the middle of the night because of the beeping from my Womb Vac machine and change it.

Frustrated and tired, I would just lay there with tears in my eyes each time she had to do it. I didn't think it would be like this. I thought that it would be better by now. These are the thoughts that continued to run through my head. When she would change my wound care, my mind would go back to when I battled cancer. I remember not having the ability to control my bowels due to cancer, and one night we were awakened out of our sleep, and I had to be carried to the shower. Completely humiliated, I told my wife to leave me. Go and find another man because you shouldn't have to care for me like this. My wife sat there and washed me while praying over me. She NEVER allowed me to feel like less of a man. This is why I cherish her forever! But fast forward 11 years later, and I'm returning to that feeling again. Why does my wife have to take care of me like this? I felt like dirt, and it only got worse.

Like clockwork, I'm popping pills left and right. I'm trying to cope with the new adjustments in my life. Twice a week, I had a wound care nurse come in and care for and change my wound. I didn't look forward to those days. I hated those days. I found myself growing bitter, and there was no way for me to stop it. Because of all the medication, I wasn't praying as often as before. I wasn't reading as much. As much as I loved people and loved being around people, I didn't want to be around people anymore. I began to think back to the days before this happened and wished I could return there. I couldn't find any peace. My mind was constantly running. I didn't have an appetite. My colostomy bag began to burst and leak, and we had a hard time figuring it out. We found a specialist who did the best she could, but it didn't work out. After going to the specialist, I got sick and vomited a lot. We couldn't figure out what was happening, so I had to return to the ER. I was becoming terrified because I thought that it was COVID. They ran some tests on me and found that I had a bug of some sort. They gave me three different medicines in the arm to try and see if that would help it go down, but it didn't. I was then informed that they would have to put me back in the hospital if I didn't get better. NO, THAT IS NOT THE NEWS I WANTED TO HEAR! The doctor then told me they had one more thing they could try. Because it was the pandemic, my wife could not be back there with me to see what they were giving me. The doctor then brings me Haloperidol, better known as Haldol. This medication is used for psych ward patients, like those with Schizophrenia, to help combat suicidal thoughts. I only found that out after I was given this medicine. We were told that it had been used for nausea. Due to the pandemic and the medication shortage, they made that choice for me. This was when my life took a turn for the worst. I returned home, and I couldn't think right to save my life. I remember hearing my wife in the other room praying and me just laying on the bed crying (I know that you guys are probably tired of hearing me repeat all of the crying, but that's all I could do). That night, I did not sleep at all. I've never experienced that a day in my life. My body and my mind were running in a million places. I went and sat on the couch in the living room, laid on the sofa in our sitting area, sat in my office, walked around the house about twenty times, and laid in my recliner; I even went outside and just stood there in my back yard looking up to heaven. I didn't say anything; I just looked. This went on for almost two weeks. I became hopeless.

I still have this bag that has to be changed and this wound vac, and now, I feel crazy. I'm still popping all this medication, and nothing seems to be helping me. Unfortunately, this is when the thoughts of suicide begin to flirt with my mind. Did I do something wrong? Is God mad at me? Why was I feeling this way? These are the thoughts that emerged in my mind day and night. One night, I got up and sat in my living room. I wanted to scream. I wanted to run outside and just scream. I rocked back and forth uncontrollably, just wanting it all to end. My wife held me, and we walked outside and began to walk up the sidewalk at 2 in the morning. We then found our way into our backyard. We sat on our bench, and my wife just held my hand, and I asked her, "What is wrong with me?" I didn't realize at the moment that the medication I was taking altered my mind and my mood. I was feeding what I was fighting. We sat outside for over an hour. I cried in my wife's arms while just praying to God. I thought that It would be better by now!

This was my expectation but not my reality. Again, I honestly believed that God was mad at me or that this was payback for something I had done in my past. Sometimes, your mind becomes like Job's friends in the moment of interruption. What did you do? The devil can't create a situation, but he will use one against you, and he was using my vulnerable state against me. The devil only attacks one area in our lives, and that's the knowledge of God.

2 Corinthians 10:5

"We are destroying sophisticated arguments and every exalted and proud thing that sets itself up against the [true] knowledge of God, and we are taking every thought and purpose captive to the obedience of Christ"

This is what the enemy does. He attacks our knowledge of God being a healer, a deliverer, and a compassionate Father. The devil attacks us by causing us to question God because of the situation that we're in currently. "If God loves you, why is this happening to you?" "If God can heal you, why are you still suffering then?" There will come a time when you will have to

> *I never stopped praying.*

wholeheartedly trust and believe in the God that you sing, dance, and preach about. This is not to say that you didn't believe Him before, but you sho nuff (I KNOW THIS ISN'T PROPER ENGLISH) gone have to believe and trust in Him now. But if the devil can get you to question a bit of what you know about God, he can deceive you. I can honestly say, as mad and frustrated as I was, I never stopped praying. It hurt, but I never stopped praying. I decided to get up and take back control of my life. I got up from that bench and began to pray over my home at four in the morning. I decreed and declared the mercy and power of God over my life. I then told my wife that I would start back preaching again. Since we were in a pandemic, preaching had shifted to online social media, which was great for me. I began preaching on Facebook; however, I shouldn't have. I wasn't ready for it, but it was the only thing I wanted to do. As I look back over everything now, I should have just rested. I wanted to jump back on because I was afraid of losing my church, and I thought they should see how a mighty man of God looks. They needed to see me strong. I needed to be the powerful man of valor, but I was far from it. I wasn't well mentally or physically. I would preach on Facebook, and my wife would have to carry me back to the bedroom afterward. I would be so frustrated! Again, I thought that I would be better by now! One day, in particular, we decided to have a small gathering at our church, and I would preach from there. Seeing some of my members would be a blessing. However, I remember crying on the way to church because I didn't get one ounce of sleep the night before. We got to the church, and it was time to put the superman cap on and the good mighty man-of-God mask. While setting up, I felt an extreme lowliness feeling. I pretended to go back to pray but went back there to cry. My wife came back there and just held me, and I cried. I asked her again, knowing she didn't have the answer, "What's wrong with me?" I thought being in the building to preach would have made me feel better. As time drew closer to go out and preach, I dried my face, put the fake smile on, and preached. As soon as the camera began to roll, I was out the gates, just preaching. Once I said the last amen of my sermon and closed my tablet, I broke down in front of my members. I cried uncontrollably, and my wife just came and wrapped her arms around me again.

I began to think, "Oh, my God, my members will think I'm soft. They are going to think that I have no faith." I sat there for about twenty minutes with my face covered in shame. However, I heard praying and intercession taking place. I lifted my head and saw that I was not alone in this fight. My members didn't see a soft preacher, and they didn't see a tough one either. They saw a human preacher. A human preacher that is not exempt from life's interruptions. I can't begin to explain how that made my heart smile a little. We sometimes hold ourselves to unrealistic standards because we think other people are holding us to those unrealistic standards. I will be honest; some people believe that men and women of God go through nothing, and if we do, we shouldn't cry. I won't say what I want to say to those people, but I will say God bless you. My wife and I left the church, drove to a little pond in Hoover, and sat looking at the water.

At that moment, I began to embrace that things may never go back to what I knew as normal, and that's okay. My mind had concluded many results for me, most of which were mere fragments of my fear, but I slowly began to see that God was with me. It felt like a breakthrough, but it was short-lived. That night I began to hurt again. My wife went to change my dressing, and I was in pain. I told her that something was wrong. I didn't get any sleep that night because of the pain. No medication worked. We called the doctor, and he told me to get to his clinic ASAP. It took my wife forty-five minutes to get me out of bed. Once we got there, he couldn't even touch my stomach. "We have to put you back in the hospital and do another procedure," he said. My heart just dropped.

Honestly, I don't want to talk about this experience. Again, the staff was great, but this was a shallow moment. I just preached the day before, and I felt like I had a breakthrough moment, and now here I am, back in the hospital. The one thing I remember from this visit was the pain medication Dilaudid. I had Dilaudid before, but this time was different. Because I have horrible veins, each time I went into the hospital, they had to give me an IV through a pic line, and all my medicine was given to me that way. I was experiencing pain from an infection that had built up in my stomach. I sunk low again. My stomach was just starting to heal, and now this. I was in much pain and was given Dilaudid to help with the pain. This opened up another door in my life. I stayed in the hospital for almost a week this time. I returned home, went back on Facebook again, and tried to act like all was well, but it wasn't. My sleep was now gone completely. I was shivering in cold sweats, and my mind was now all over the place, worse than before. I couldn't focus and couldn't understand why I wasn't getting better. I just wanted to go back to normal. The ambulance lived at my house because of all the complications with my body. They had to come to my house once because my body had gone into shock, and my wife had to slap me back to reality. I had lost all mobility, and the ambulance came and helped me up off the floor. This is when I begin to see my wife cry. She was strong through everything but thought she had lost me at that moment. It broke my heart. Again, all I could do was cry and pray. I fell deeper into depression, and there was no way to hide it. I remember my wife grabbing my hand and telling me, "Please don't give up on me." That was a challenging moment. I don't want to knock on medication, but the majority of what I went through was because of medication. We had to go and get some prescriptions filled, and I remember reading the side effects of this particular pill, and it read "sorrow and sadness" was one of the side effects. I told my wife, "I'm not taking this anymore," and I quit cold turkey. That was the worst idea ever because my body had become so used to it, and quitting cold turkey was horrible, and I paid for it. I don't recommend anyone doing that. Please get proper help and insight from your doctor about what you desire to do. I was progressively growing towards addiction to all the medication, and I just wanted to give up on life. Mental battles and depression had become strong in my life. I was given more medicine for depression and sleep. They honestly just made me numb. My parents would come over and pray for me, and my cousins Jerome and Thandi Wells, both therapists, would talk me through my struggling moments. (They introduced me to my current therapist, who is fantastic) My sister would coach me through some of my down days. My spiritual parents would call and pray and encourage me. But honestly, nothing that anyone said made sense at that moment. The day I remember the most was when my wife had to return to work. That day was the first time since my surgery that I would be left alone at home. I had prayed hard the night before and had already planned all I would do to keep my mind occupied the next day. I would get up that morning and pray, clean up the house and sit outside with the birds. NONE OF IT WORKED! I woke up that morning in tears for no apparent reason. My bedroom walls seemed to start closing in, and there was nothing I could do. My wife called and checked on me, and I tried to sound as if I was good, but she could tell that I had been crying. She wanted to come home, but I told her not to. I got up from the bed and pushed myself to do something. I tried cleaning up around the house, but that didn't work. I took my medication and found myself on the floor in my living room, sitting with my legs crossed, just crying. My wife called me again; this time, I couldn't hide my tears. After I got off the phone with her, a great friend/brother, Pastor Derrick Morrissette, called me, and I accidentally hit the answer button; he heard me crying, and he shot straight over. Derrick and my wife just sat on the floor with me and prayed. We sat there for an hour, and I said again, "I thought I would be better by now." Sometimes people don't need you to come and preach to or at them; they just need someone to come and just sit and listen. I just knew that everything would be better, but it wasn't. That same evening we found out the most crippling news, my spiritual grandfather had passed, Apostle Maurice K. Wright. I couldn't believe it. I just sat there and looked at the wall. This was the man that had just called me a few weeks ago and told me that everything would be okay, and now he's gone. I had no more tears to cry at this point. All I could say was, "God, I trust you." I know that I have just shared a lot of depressing parts here, and I honestly feel some way for sharing it all. Although I have shared all of this, one thing I want you to know is that God was with me through it all, and He is with you as well. I read something Dr. Tony Evans had written: "Sometimes God lets you hit rock bottom so that you will discover that He is the rock at the bottom." Don't you dare allow the enemy to consume your mind and make you feel as if your situation can't get better. The devil is a LIAR! God isn't just with you on the boat of life but also in the sea. He doesn't pack up His bags and leave when life becomes a shock to us. NO! He stands right there with us. When Moses saw the Red Sea in front of him and Pharaoh's army behind him, he became distraught, NOT GOD! He knew the outcome; Moses didn't. He knows our outcome!

The problem is, we don't. We know He will bring us through; we just don't know when. Moses saw a sea; God saw a dry path in the ocean. Please don't try and figure God out because you won't. That only makes matters of life worse. The whole world is in God's hands, not ours, and we must trust that He has us in His hands. An acronym the Holy Spirit gave me years ago about H.A.N.D.S was, His Authority, Nature, and Divine Spirit, and He has us in all of these.

John 10:29 ESV

My Father, who has given them to me, is greater than all, and no one is able to snatch them out of the Father's hand.

Life will try and snatch you out of God's hands. Depression will try and grab you out of God's hands. Anger will push and snatch you out of God's hands. They won't succeed because our God is greater than them ALL! I know it hurts right now, but it will get better. The devil will employ your pain to work against you; God will use it to work for you (Romans 8:31). Isaiah 54:17 says that the weapon that's formed against you won't prosper, but it doesn't say that it wouldn't penetrate. Troubles have a way of penetrating our hearts, minds, and souls, but they won't kill us. It doesn't mean that you won't hurt; it just means that you won't die. One of the ways that God helped me was I was introduced to an amazing therapist that God used. One of the things I had to learn to let go of was my expectations of everyday life. I needed to let go of what I thought my life should look like and embrace where I was at that moment. I let go and began to walk the journey of healing. I created a place of peace in my backyard. A bird sanctuary, if you will. I would sit out from sun up to sun down and watch these birds. My mother purchased a bird feeder for me, and I bought more bird feeders and hummingbird feeders. I bought birdbaths and transformed my entire backyard into my sanctuary. That's the place where God begins to meet me. I had, and we still have, over 20 different species of birds in my backyard, and they were my little buddies. I even downloaded an app to identify what kind of birds they were. In particular, one that met my wife and me every morning and evening was this beautiful red bird. I will talk about them later on, but you will be amazed at what God uses to bring you peace. You see, different interruptions require new methods of serenity. My wife and I were blessed with a labradoodle from a lady on Facebook who followed our story. This is by far the craziest dog ever, but I love him to life. We got him home, and my friend/brother George

> *You will be amazed at what God uses to bring you peace.*

Yielder helped us name him Bishop after a comic character. That dog helped bring a great balance into our now-interrupted life. I finally found myself smiling again. God began to teach me about life and how to flow with it through different methods that I never knew before. Developing patience with yourself was something that I had to learn to do. When life slowly turned for the better, it kept turning for the better. I got approved for a reversal on my colostomy bag, and I couldn't have been more excited. However, I would be lying if I told you that I didn't feel complete anxiety about the reversal. I joined a Colostomy/Ileostomy Group on Facebook, which was a blessing and a curse. People wrote about their experiences with the reversal. Some were good reports, but most of them weren't so good. I almost didn't want to get it, but I praise God that I went through it.

"The Christian life is not a constant high. I have my moments of deep discouragement. I have to go to God in prayer with tears in my eyes and say, 'O God, forgive me,' or 'Help me.'"

Billy Graham

CHAPTER V
Hard Pressed but NOT Destroyed

2 Corinthians 4:8-9

We are hard pressed on every side, but not crushed; perplexed, but not in despair; persecuted, but not abandoned; struck down, but not destroyed.

One of the challenges of interruptions in life is focusing on our current reality and not our faith. Paul makes a statement in the above verses that gives his present reality and faith. We are hard-pressed (Reality), but we're not crushed (Faith). We are perplexed (Reality), but we're not in despair (Faith). We often see our present situations clearly, yet the faith is on a distant shore. The struggle of faith is that it's not seen. Faith isn't to be seen but to be lived. 2 Corinthians 5:7, "For we walk by faith, and not by sight." Our stance on our faith may not line up with the condition of what we see and feel. By faith, we know that we are healed, but our current condition is sickness, which challenges us. What I think and believe is in complete opposition, and my sanity hinges on whether I choose to go with what I believe or succumb to what I think. The good news is that you will not be destroyed no matter which direction you go. That pain, discomfort, depression, etc., are real, but that's not the end of your story. Faith is still writing our story even while you may be crying. Another statement Paul makes within the scripture above is, "Hard Pressed on every side." What do you do when there's trouble in every direction you turn? If it's not your health, it's your home. If it's not your home, it's your children. If it's not the children, it's your spouse, job, finances, etc. However, Job gives a good answer to this question: Job 13:15 -"Yet will I trust Him." This is what I had to remind myself during this next phase of my life. After having a few good weeks, I was excited to have my reversal done. The day before my reversal, I went to Alabama Adult/Teen Challenge, a fantastic addiction/rehab facility at which I have the honor to teach. I have been going there for over six years every first and third Monday, and it's such a blessing to see these men and women overcome what had tried to overcome them. After a fantastic time at ATC, I had my first complete blowout from my bag on my way home. My family came over, sat outside on our porch, and I had another blowout. (Gross Moment if you want to skip) A blowout is where your colostomy bag falls entirely from your body, and you get the picture. Everything in it comes out of it and onto everything around you. I became frustrated again, but I reminded myself that I was in God's hands and didn't allow this to pull me from my place of peace. Outside of the blowout, the night before was a lovely summer evening. We just had that good old Alabama summer evening rain, and the sky was a pretty baby blue-pinkish color with a few strokes of white faded clouds. I remember it so well because I stared up at the sky, remembering that just a few weeks ago, I was out there looking up at a pitch-black sky with no hope. I didn't sleep that night but learned to be okay with that. My biggest battle with sleep was forcing myself to go to sleep. I was taught not to force myself to sleep but find something to do when I couldn't sleep. I found things to do like reading a book, praying, watching a movie (Grown Ups had become my go-to movie, don't ask me why), or going and playing a video game. (Still A Big Kid) I did anything that helped relax my mind and bring me peace. However, this particular night I was up thinking about the surgery. My mind was going over what they were going to do to me. The reversal is where they reattach your intestine and allow your bowels to flow as they once did before.

They were also going to close up my stomach. I tried my best not to play out the next day in my head, but I couldn't. Being that we were in a pandemic, they weren't allowing visitors. However, I praise God for my therapist and cousin writing me a letter stating that it wasn't good for me to be alone and that my wife needed to be with me because I had fallen in my mental health. My doctor also approved Salisia to be with me through all procedures. I couldn't praise God enough because I knew that I wouldn't have been able to make it through this procedure without her by my side. We arrived at the hospital the following day, and, as before, all of the staff knew us. It was like we had become a distant family of sorts. When we got back in the back, we said our prayers and just waited. Let me tell you something! That felt like the

> *That's where the devil gets most of us, in the wait.*

most extended wait ever, and that's where the devil gets most of us, IN THE WAIT. The wait, when in anticipation, can become a weight on our minds. It's a place of uncertainty. You have no control over the situation, although you would like it to move NOW! I didn't have enough games to play on my phone to keep my attention. We watched some weird show about cheap people on TV, it was crazy, but that only lasted for a few moments. I looked at Facebook so much that I felt like I knew everyone's problems, birthdays, anniversaries, and what they had for breakfast that morning.

However, nothing was able to keep my attention from the surgery. Finally, the door opened, and we were off to the Operating Room. Again, I knew everyone in the OR room because I had been there so much. I didn't mention some of those times in this book because it was too much. I asked them if I could pray with them before the procedure, and I praised God that my doctor was a believer and allowed us to do so. After prayer, all I remember was them placing that breathing cup over my nose and hello, goodbye, gone – Off to La La Land. Of course, after they put you to sleep, it feels like only two seconds have passed. I woke up to my wife's beautiful smile, and she was holding my hand. From there, I knew that all was well. The Colostomy bag was gone, and my stomach had been closed back up. However, I now have some crazy-looking device on my stomach that scarred me because I thought I was stuck with something else; it was another form of a wound vac to help keep infections down. I was in pain, getting Dilaudid every two hours while having the pain pump. I went to town on that machine because I was in great pain, and it helped for the moment. The next day comes around and in walks my PT nurse from day one. I knew what she was going to say, and I was ready to Get Up! I was only able to stand this time, but I got up. I felt stronger each day, but I was still in pain.

We were waiting on my insides (intestines) to wake up, and it seemed like it took forever for that to happen. A week goes by, and the doctors finally hear some rumbling in my stomach, but I'm still in pain. I told my wife that something didn't feel right and I was not feeling well. I had no strength to get out of bed for the next two days. All I was feeling was pain. I felt myself slowly starting to fade into the place of worrying. All I could think about was the last time I was in the hospital. The doctor ordered me to get a cat scan, and they found that my intestine had a leak. NOT AGAIN! I had to go back to the OR so they could put a drain in my stomach to help drain the fluid from within my intestine. As I was wheeled back into the operating room, my reality overtook my mind. I didn't know what was happening, nor did I know if I would make it out alive or not. I begin to lean on my faith in God. There was nothing I could do but trust Him. My reality was looking different from my faith. I felt every bit of the pain in my body and the sickness within my stomach. I didn't understand this current situation, and I had to stop my mind from searching for answers I knew I couldn't find. I just had to trust God. I began to decree, "I'm not going to die here!" I looked at my wife and told her, "I'm not going to die here!" That was my confession, and I was going to stick to it. A few days had now passed, and still no movement. It's been going on for two weeks now. My wife and I began to pray, and I just asked God to make something happen, and He did. My bowels woke up the next day, and I was so excited and grateful, but I was still in pain. I figured it was from getting up and walking along with the recovery. I kept getting Dilaudid every two hours. I had gone through many things up to this point, but the situation finally started to shift for good. I was given a release date and couldn't have been happier. The day had come for me to be released. My wife packed the bags, and we talked the night before about returning home and all the things we would do. However, I began to get nauseated. I got worried, but I knew that everything would be okay. The doctor came in, and we were ready to hit the road. He went to my drain, saw nothing else coming out of it, and said, "Let's take it out." Finally, I thought to myself, some good news upon good news. He counted to three and pulled the tube out, but the end of the line was pig-tailed, which meant it was curled inside of me and cut on the way out. I screamed to the top of my lungs in agony. My wife's eyes, the nurse's eyes, and the doctor's eyes became huge. They quickly patched me up, and I was utterly disappointed because I knew I wasn't about to go anywhere. They ended up giving me two extra doses of Dilaudid after that. I remember looking at the clock, and It was around 10 am after receiving that dose, and I didn't wake up until about 6 pm that evening. I woke up to my wife wiping tears from her eyes and praying. I grabbed her hand and told her, "I'm not going to die here! God's got us!" We planned the night before to be at our home watching movies around this time, but here we are, still stuck in the hospital. I had lost my appetite, and I had no desire for anything. My body had begun to reject anything that I was given. To try and keep my strength up, my wife and I would walk the halls of that hospital three times a day, at least ten laps a day, but I was still hurting. I became disappointed because something would happen to keep me in every time I was given a release date. My wife and I prayed so much in that room that every nurse who entered our room never wanted to leave. There were times that we found ourselves ministering to them. Because of the pandemic and the stress they had to endure, they would tell us how refreshing and peaceful it was just to sit there. God even allowed me the opportunity to lead one of them back to Christ. Those nurses had real battles outside that hospital, and I understood that all too well. The majority of the people that are helpers and encouragers in life are the ones that need the most help and encouragement. So I understood how they were feeling. Some would cry, some would vent, and some would just take a breath from the day.

I must say, the entire staff at Shelby Baptist Medical Center was fantastic. They took exceptional care of my wife and me. They all were a blessing.

While in the hospital, my sister was housesitting and babysitting our new fur baby, Bishop. Unfortunately, she caught Covid, which scared us to death because we had no clue what this meant for her life. After watching all of this on the news and hearing about the people in the hospital dying from this, I became afraid for her, and there was no way we could get to her or see her. We were also scared because we didn't know what that meant for our home. We knew we couldn't return home with my current condition and not fully understanding everything about Covid. Fortunately, some awesome church members went to our home and cleaned and sanitized our entire house. My wife had purchased a new bed that needed to be assembled, and my good friend/brother Pastor Derrick Morrisette and some of his men came and assembled our new bed, disassembled our old mattress, and took everything out. I was beyond grateful because the whole time I was worried about losing my church, the church was at my house taking care of everything. My church went above and beyond for us. We thank God that my sister fully recovered from Covid. We got another release date. Praise God! On the day I was to be released, I began to feel nauseated again. (GROSS MOMENT) We called the nurse to the room and asked her for one of the bags made for vomit. As soon as she handed me the bag, there it went. After I threw up, I noticed an odd smell. I looked down and saw that I had just thrown up stool. It came out of both ends. I just sat there. Numb to everything. I didn't care at this moment. I had not a feeling left within me. My reality was getting the best of me, and my faith had started to fade, but I told God, "I trust you." I was rushed down to the OR again, but they couldn't put me to sleep this time. They had to put another drain within me, which had to happen at that moment. They held a sheet over my head, and I felt the needles injecting the numbing medicine. I remember looking up towards the light, thinking to myself, why? I felt every bit of the tube going into my intestine and clenched my fist in anger. It was at that moment of weakness that the devil tried me. You're the Bishop; why would God treat you this way? You have prayed for many, but no one is praying for you? Just let it go! I would be lying if the thought of letting go didn't cross my mind, but I chose to rejoice. With tears in my eyes, all I could hear was the song, "Precious Lord, take my hand, lead me on, help me stand. I am tired, I am weak, I am worn; through the storm, through the night, Lead me on to the light". I hummed this song the entire time. I refused to let my faith shake, but this was hard. I was disappointed, but I was not disapproved. God's favor was still on me. Although I felt the pain, I chose to believe that God was still with me. Just like He's with you! Again, God never promised us any days without trouble. But He did promise us that there would be no days without Him. A Scripture that the Holy Spirit led me to think about was Habakkuk 3:17-19:

> "Even though the fig trees have no blossoms, and there are no grapes on the vines; even though the olive crop fails, and the fields lie empty and barren; even though the flocks die in the fields, and the cattle barns are empty, yet I will rejoice in the Lord! I will be joyful in the God of my salvation! The Sovereign Lord is my strength! He makes me as surefooted as a deer, able to tread upon the heights."

I chose to sing my way back to my room, and my transporter hummed right along with me. I now had another tube in my body, and I just chose to keep believing in God. My therapist taught me to think about my life's happy moments and days and dwell on those days. When I got back to my room, I found my wife praying. I told her again, "I will not die here!" I lay there in my room and began thinking about sitting in my backyard and all the birds back there. I learned of many of them, but a few would always stick out to me. There was the Eastern Towhee, The Red Bird, The Dove, and this little yellow bird that I couldn't figure out. I told my wife what I was thinking about, and we sat in that room looking at the birds in our minds and our crazy dog Bishop running around chasing the Squirrels. The following day we woke up to a pecking sound on the window, and you know what it was, an Eastern Towhee Bird. We hadn't seen one up there until that morning. My wife and I just looked at each other and laughed. My wife then jumped up and pointed into the tree, and three Mourning Doves were sitting in the tree. To top it all off, two red birds came and perched on the brick wall. We cried tears of joy because although we didn't

> *God will sometimes show you that He's with you rather than tell you*

hear God's voice, we heard Him loud and clear through those birds. God will sometimes show you that He's with you rather than tell you. A week went by, and I could get that tube out, and I was beginning to feel a little better. The day finally came when I could go home. My reversal surgery was on June 10th, and I was now going home on July 4th. Everything had finally gone the way we wanted it to go. No complications, no hiccups. FINALLY! I wrote on Facebook that I was finally going home. Everyone was so excited, and we were too. We got loaded up to go home, and off we went. Grateful, but that was short-lived. As soon as we got home, I began to crash. My body started shutting down, and I was scared to death. My wife had to slap me back to consciousness, and all I could do was look up towards the ceiling. Again, what is wrong with me? I asked. My wife walked me to the bedroom, and I saw the beautiful orange covers that our members had made our bed, along with the brand-new mattress. I lay on the bed, and my wife turned on the television. Four movies played that night that I can't watch to this day: Saving Private Ryan, The Upside, Thor, and Battleship. Those movies have become a trigger for me. The mind is mighty. I walked to my porch the next day and began watching the birds. My wife came outside, and I told her something didn't feel right. I'm still in pain. We sat there for about an hour, and I told her my pain had worsened. We had to call the ambulance. I could barely walk from the backyard to the kitchen. When I got to the kitchen, I collapsed. The ambulance came and loaded me up, and this was when I was introduced to another powerful drug called, Ketamine, better known as special K, on the street. Because I'm a big guy, they had to shoot me up with the most significant dose they could give, and MAN! I don't know how or why anyone would want to take that drug on purpose. I was hallucinating like crazy, and it scared me. I can laugh about this now, but I was high as a kite. I started prophesying to the driver and the woman back there with me. All jokes aside, I thought I was in a looney toon movie, and she was goofy.

When we got to the hospital, they saw that I had a high fever, and being that it was a pandemic, I had to sit outside until they tested me negative for Covid. I was then rushed to the CT, and another pocket was found in my intestine. I was at my breaking point. I cried in that ER room like a baby. When will it end? My wife had found this song on YouTube that I believe God made specifically for me. It was called "Never Lost A Battle," sung by Candler Moore and Holly. We repeated that song and set an atmosphere of worship in that ER room. Don't ever allow trials to stop your worship. The devil tried to shut my ear up from hearing heaven, but that wasn't going to happen. Remember, a closed off ear to God is an open ear to the devil. We have to learn how to pray in good and challenging conditions. 1 Samuel 15: 10 says that: Hannah was greatly distressed, and she prayed to the Lord and wept in anguish. Hannah prayed not only from the place of distress, but she also wept in anguish. Jesus prayed with blood streaming down His face, which was a medical condition caused by stress. We must understand that prayer is what we do in the good and the bad times. It's in the moments of anguish that real prayer is birthed. Not that rehearsed prayer that you've prayed for all your life. Suffering has a way of birthing prayer not just from your mouth but from your tears. While we were praying, the doctor walked back in and told us that they would have to readmit me. My heart sunk within me, but we kept on singing. I was then told I would have to get another procedure to remove the pocket. I felt the frustration rising, but we just kept on worshipping. Let me be honest. I know I'm writing about us continuing to sing and pray, but this was extremely HARD TO DO! We had so many emotions running through us, and I was tired. But I looked at my wife and told her that this would NOT beat me! While we were speaking, a nurse walked into our room. She was very quiet, but I knew something was up about her. She then grabbed my hand, looked at my wife, and said, "The Lord told me to tell you both that you will be okay. You're in His hands." We just wept because of all the praying I was doing, and I would be lying if I told you I felt God. I didn't feel Him while I was praying. I felt pain. I felt rage. I felt neglected. I felt less of a man and less of a leader. That's what I felt. But when I heard her say that, my spirit leaped. I was in pain but was also at peace. God had worked it out so that we ended up right back in the same room I was just released from the day before. As they wheeled me back to the room, some of the nurses' mouths dropped, and they even began to cry. They knew that we didn't want to be back up there. I refused to stay in that bed and walked those halls that night. One of the nurses there was named Maurice, and when he saw us walking, he told us, "And this too shall pass." All we could do was walk, praise, and cry. We didn't want any pity, and we didn't want anybody feeling sorry for us, but this was hard. The following day I woke up to the sound of crying. My wife had finally reached her breaking point. She was so strong through all of this, but she just broke. We began to pray, and while we were praying, an echo tech came in to check the function of my heart because I had been passing out and was extremely weak. While she was checking my heart, the transporter came to get me to take me back to surgery. Before they moved me, God showed up again. I looked out the window and saw two Red Birds sitting there looking at us. I knew we were going to be okay, but it still hurt. I praise God for the tech because she went and just hugged my wife as they wheeled me out. My wife is a strong woman, but God knew she needed that Angel with her at that moment. I heard her crying down the hall as they wheeled me to the operating room. As I was heading down, I felt something cold beside me. I can't describe what I saw or felt, but it looked and felt like death. It had no appearance at all, but it felt like death. They sat me in the waiting area, and it was just gloomy. I can't lie; I thought that I was about to die. This was another procedure in which they couldn't put me to sleep, and again, although they used numbing medicine, I felt everything. They lifted a white sheet, and I could hear and feel what they were doing. I just begin to sing Precious Lord and decree, "I will not DIE!" The presence of that figure began to fade away slowly. One of the nurses saw me crying and thought I was crying because I could feel what they were doing. My reply to her was, "These are tears of just being tired." She grabbed my hand and began to pray, and I felt the peace of God. I still felt His peace with tears in my eyes and pain in my body.

After receiving this drain, I had to go on what is known as bowel rest, and I was placed on Total Parental Nutrition. I had lost a substantial amount of weight, and my body began to shock. My body was in a state of anorexia. I went in at 384 pounds, and I was down to 282. I was then visited by a Psychiatrist that wanted to put me on more medication to help me with the depression. I told them I didn't want it; I just wanted to see my family and friends. Sometimes it's not the medication that helps but seeing people. I am a people person, and I missed my family. God must have heard me because my parents drove past my window and held up signs of encouragement for my wife and me the next day. My wife had some of my friends and family send encouragement through Facebook, text messages, etc. The staff also allowed brief visitation from two of my brothers/friends, Bishop Sylvester Mixon and

Pastor Derrick Morrisette. While Pastor Derrick was there, the doctor came in and delivered more bad news about my health. It got the best of me then, but I pushed my way out. I told my wife I would not go home with drains or a TPN bag. God heard my prayer, and my health began to turn for the better. As the days went by, I got medication around the clock and Dilaudid. One particular night, I walked around the unit, and one of the nurses asked me if I needed any pain medication. I remember telling her no thank you; however, I began to shiver uncontrollably, getting to my room and lying in my bed. I quickly called for her to bring the medicine to me and my body quickly calmed down. I didn't understand at the moment what was happening, but soon enough, I would find out what was happening to me. I was finally able to get released from the hospital on July 16th. I had spent almost two months in that hospital, and the battles

God had helped me conquer were nothing short of a miracle. Life definitely tried to kill me this go-round in the hospital, but God. I felt things and dealt with things I never imagined, but God. Through all of this, God showed himself faithful and true. There were moments when I didn't think I would make it, but my story is still being written, and so is yours.

"Pressure does two things, it can break, and it can create. Both are beneficial; it just depends on whose hands it's in."

Dr. Maurice Valentine

CHAPTER VI
ADDICTION

1 Corinthians 10:13

No temptation has overtaken you that is not common to man. God is faithful, and he will not let you be tempted beyond your ability, but with the temptation, he will also provide the way of escape, that you may be able to endure.

I must admit that I took a few months away from writing the following few chapters of this book because I could not deal with the mental battles that came from reliving and typing my journey from last year. I thank God for His Spirit to help me continue. I know that some have gone through much worse, and my heart is with you; I pray that you will one day share your story of how you made it through. Please don't stop, and don't allow yourself nor insecurities to block you from sharing your story. So now I continue writing this book. When I returned home from the hospital, I didn't know what to expect or realize what I was about to face. I didn't want to get excited because I didn't want to get let down again with something happening to me. I remember walking into the house and standing in my doorway somewhat in a daze. I was happy and yet confused at the same time. The first night home was torture. I didn't sleep; I tossed and turned throughout the night, which had become my norm at home. I was up and down throughout the night with chills running up and down my body. I had developed a restless leg, and I would shiver and move uncontrollably in my bed. I would unintentionally wake my wife up, and she would have to hold me as tight as she could to calm me down. I found myself going to sleep crying and waking up crying for no apparent reason. I sat in a fetal position either in my bedroom or outside with my birds. I found no strength to do anything but just lay around and cry, and then it happened; sharp pain in my side. In a panic, I looked at my wife and told her something wasn't right, and we returned to the hospital. By now, the people knew everything about me and knew my story. My wife was able to go in, and as they laid me on the bed, they asked me what my pain level was, and I told them. They then gave me a shot of, you guessed it, Dilaudid. As soon as I received it, a warm and calming feeling came over me, and I was fine. They took me down for tests, and everything came back fine. The doctor told me that I had been on the discussion table of many doctors there, and he knew my story and said to me,

"You're healing, and everything looks good." My wife went out and talked to them, and while she was gone, another nurse came in and gave me another dose of pain meds. I went home that night and slept like a baby until I was awakened by the sounds of wheels rolling on the floor, but nothing was there. I heard the clicking sound of a door, and I looked to see what it was, and it was nothing. I sat in bed feeling like I was back in the hospital. This experience was at 2 in the morning. When I woke up the next day, I woke to the new norm of crying. I sat in bed, put my head in my hands, and felt like crap. I honestly wanted to die. I heard those sounds again, and I began to feel crazy. I was too weak to walk. My wife came and helped me outside, where I just sat and watched the birds fly and eat the leftover bird feed. I sat outside for about 5-6 hours that day. I had no appetite or desire to do anything but sit there. My body was trembling, and I didn't know why. I was sick to my stomach, and the thought of food made me sick. I would even vomit with nothing coming out. My wife sat with me, trying to figure out what to say, and there was nothing she could say. I just wanted to let go. I felt like a burden to her, and I became angry with myself for a situation I had no control over. My wife called my parents over, hoping to cheer me up, and it did for a moment, but depression, nausea, and hopelessness returned with a vengeance. I sat in my chair in our living room and remembered hearing the sound of doors opening and rolling wheels from a cart on the floor. I then looked at the clock on my wall, and it hit me. It was 4 o'clock at that moment. When I was in the hospital, they gave me, at my request, Dilaudid every two hours around the clock. I got it at 12 o'clock, 2 o'clock, 4 o'clock, 6 o'clock, etc. When I called for it, I could hear the cart of my nurse coming, and when they walked into my room, they had to click my door to enter, which were the noises I was hearing. My body had adjusted to the around-the-clock medication I was no longer getting, and I was going through withdrawal from the pain medication. I then knew that I had become addicted to this pain medication, which was a massive fear of mine.

I remember getting up and telling my wife, "I'm addicted to Dilaudid." My wife had this look of relief across her face that confused the mess out of me. She knew. She knew what I was battling and had been praying for me. She knew what I was facing when I went to the E.R. When she left my E.R. room that night; she told the nurses that I had become addicted. She told them not to give me any more medicine, but they still gave it to me. (I don't fault them at all for that, I asked for it) However, my wife knew. The next few weeks were HORRIBLE! I never felt what I felt in my life. Cold sweats, nausea, insomnia, hallucinations, the desire to die, depression, anxiety, and no comfort or peace. I walked within my home without direction and was numb to everything. I would sit in my backyard late at night and cry because I wanted another shot. My flesh would try to find a reason to return to the hospital. The lie I told myself is just one more shot, and I'll be okay. I knew that if I got that shot, it wouldn't quench the desire for more. That's what addiction does. It tells you just one more drink, one more shot, one more look at porn, just one more time, and that's it. It's never it if you continue to feed into it. I became honest with my wife, therapist, family, and pastor. It's so important to be honest with yourself. Was I ashamed? Yes! I was embarrassed because I wanted it. I was craving the medication, and here I am, a Bishop, craving something more than God. I never thought that something could bring such a battle within my life that would cause me to sit and figure out ways of obtaining it. The Holy Spirit helped me to overcome pornography years ago. I'm a part of an accountability group called Covenant Eyes, God over Porn, and other groups that I work within as well as follow. (Not ashamed to admit it) But this battle was different. I had every pill for pain, but none could give me that high, which was highly frustrating. Over six months, my body had been introduced to many forms of medication, from Ketamine (I hallucinated horribly), Haldol, Compazine (which gave me severe hallucinations), and over 30 different pills I took daily. Still, none could get me to that place of Dilaudid. How did you overcome it? Again, I became honest with myself. Paul says in Romans 7:24-25: O

> *I became honest with myself.*

wretched man that I am! Who will deliver me from this body of death? I thank God—through Jesus Christ our Lord!

Paul didn't say, "Oh wretched man that you are!" But Paul said, "Oh wretched man that I am!" You have to look at the person in the mirror instead of the person around it and realize that you need help, and that's what I had to do. I realized I was not strong enough to handle this alone, just like the first addiction. I don't care how educated and knowledgeable you are; there is a battle that you can't preach yourself free from fighting. You can't sing your way out of it, nor can you calculate your way out of it. You need a savior whose name is Jesus, and Jesus can't become a savior to someone who refuses to be honest with who they are and acknowledge that they need a savior. I opened up to my wife and therapist, and they began to help me cope with what I was going through. I told myself that I refused to become a slave to this medication. I fought, and I prayed. I cried, and I prayed. I screamed, and I prayed. I talked with my therapist, and I prayed. I read my word, and I prayed. I punched a pillow, and I prayed. I didn't stop praying, and I refused to give in. I felt like I was coming out of a battle in the hospital into a struggle within my home with this medication. I read many books on fighting addiction and scriptures that dealt with this issue, just like the one above in the opening of this chapter. 1 Corinthians 10:13 - No temptation has overtaken you that is not common to man.

God is faithful, and he will not let you be tempted beyond your ability, but with the temptation, he will also provide the way of escape, that you may be able to endure. There is no addiction on this earth that someone else hasn't conquered. Life will sometimes make you feel like you're the only one dealing with this battle and no one else understands you. Someone has not only fought this battle, but someone else has overcome this battle. Struggles and addictions are meant to be won and overcome! They are not meant to become a part of your everyday life, but they are intended to become a part of your overcoming testimony. Please don't allow the addiction to make itself a permanent roommate in your life. God always provides a way of escape; however, we sometimes don't like the escape route He gives us. The escape door out of the addiction room can be a rehab facility, therapy, opening up to your TRUE loved ones, or returning to church. When you're in a burning building, and the stairwell is on fire, and the elevator is engulfed in flames, and the Fire Department says that the only way out the building is through the window, you don't have the option of saying how you would like to be rescued. You have to take the opportunity given. Firefighters are prepared to catch you and not let you fall, but you have to jump. You have to trust the arms that you're jumping into, and that's not always easy, but in this case, it's necessary for your survival, and it's in that moment when a choice must be made. Do I jump or die in this place because I don't like the option I've been given?

Now I know this was a pretty dramatic example; however, many people are trapped in the apartment of their minds, surrounded by addictions. They refuse to jump into the arms of help and are slowly succumbing to a life of imprisonment because they don't like the escape route. The enemy loves people like this. Denial and isolation are food to addiction; once the addiction happens, isolation is the devil's playground. Isolation makes every battle and addiction seem impossible to conquer. I love lions. I love them primarily because Christ is the Lion of the Tribe of Judah. I love watching animal planet; they did a documentary on lions, and

I was highly intrigued to watch and learn more about the lives of lions. Well, I found that the nature of a lion is pretty raw. But one thing that stood out to me was their method of hunting. The lioness is the primary hunter for the tribe. They will wait patiently while stalking their prey. They will hide patiently and blend in with their surroundings while watching their prey graze with no earthly idea that they're being watched. One method that the lion uses is the startling method. Once the lion has its target set, the lion pops up from the bushes and startles and scares the prey. The prey, in turn, panics, runs away from the herd, becomes isolated, and plays right into the hand of the lion. Isolation for a single lion is very beneficial. Isolation takes the prey away from its help and protection. A herd of buffalo can kill and has killed a single lion. Lions are afraid of a pack that sticks together, but one that isolates itself is pretty much a menu special for the night. And this is the same tactic that the devil uses. Peter says in 1Peter 5:8 (b)-The devil, your enemy, goes around like a roaring lion looking for someone to devour.

> *The devil will watch you ... waiting for the right opportunity.*

The devil will watch you for hours, days, or months if need be, waiting for the right opportunity to devour you. It's not always the devil that startles us, but life. When life surprises us, we begin to run in a panic and find ourselves isolated from family, friends, church, etc. At this moment, the enemy sees a great opportunity to devour you. Now he doesn't devour you quickly but slowly through the grip of alcohol, pornography, drugs, work (Yes, work can become an addiction), shopping, etc. Addiction is not there to help you but to devour you. It consumes your mind, your marriage, your joy, your confidence, your peace, your relationships with your loved ones, etc. Addiction, just like a lion, doesn't care if you're black, white, rich, poor, big, tall, etc. If it's hungry and you're available, it will devour you. However, there is always an escape. Mine was through therapy, prayer, family, and facing the man in the mirror and letting him know that you will not destroy this life, nor will you devour my mind, body, and soul. This is an everyday declaration. Here's another way I overcame. I work with a fantastic rehab facility called Alabama Adult/Teen Challenge, and I have been working with them for over six years. I have the privilege of watching these men and women of God turn their lives around through this program. A few of my church members are graduates of this fantastic program. I would hear them share their stories and battles, and my heart always went out to them and for them. I would go and preach to them with all that I had to give; however, I never fully understood the demons they faced and the battles they had to endure within their mind until I went through this battle. I would sit and listen to their stories and learn from them. Don't ever get so big in life that you feel you can't learn from someone because they don't have the same title as you. I praise God for these amazing men and women of God and their stories. They have been a more significant help to me through their stories than I could have ever been to them. I now preach to them with a different fire than before. I now understand what they have gone through and want them to know, as well as you reading this, that there is no addiction stronger than God's love, and there's no addiction more powerful than a made-up mind to be free. Don't be ashamed of what you're going through. You're not alone, my brother. You're not alone, my sister. Take the escape of life; you're worth it. The following chapters will hopefully encourage you to deal with life's disappointments.

"If you can't fly, then run. If you can't run, then walk.

If you can't walk, crawl, but whatever you do,

you have to keep moving forward."

Martin Luther King Jr.

CHAPTER VII
DEALING WITH DISAPPOINTMENTS

The definition of disappointment is simply discouragement – a loss of courage or enthusiasm – from something not going your way or an unexpected happening that alters the viewpoint of your day and life. One thing we must understand about life is that it's full of sunny and rainy days. You may have days of pure joy and days of pure frustration. One moment is full of heavenly bliss, and the next is full of sorrow because of a phone call that wasn't pleasant or an unexpected event. This is called Life. No matter how much we hope that our lives are never interrupted by the news of death, the challenges of sickness, the struggles with our children, the stress of work, etc. This journey is a path of mountains, hills, and valleys, and if we're going to get to the end of it, we're going to have to run, walk, or crawl through the sunny days and the rainy ones. However, this is not always easy to do. One thing I appreciate about the ministry of Jesus Christ is that He never lied to us. I think the church today has focused so much on messages about blessings, name it and claim it, and decree a thing, that the church is shocked and confused when trials and tribulations come. Some Christians don't know how to handle the challenges of life. Don't get me wrong, I believe that we should know about the blessings and favor of God, but Christ taught from a place of balance of prosperity and trials of life. If Christ focused on one topic more than the other, it was not prosperity but suffering. The suffering that He had to endure and the suffering that we will endure. Peter teaches us, 1 Peter 4:12, "Beloved, think it not strange concerning the fiery trial which is to try you, as though some strange thing happened unto you." We're not supposed to be surprised when trials come; however, we are. We're supposed to understand that trials are a part of life, just like tests are a part of a school, and the truth is, no one likes tests in school, just like none of us like tests in life. However, just like a school test, tests in life can mature you to the next level of understanding. Jesus says this in Mark 10:30 - "but he shall receive a hundredfold now in this time, houses and brethren and sisters and mothers and children and lands, with

> *Tests in life can mature you to the next level of understanding.*

persecutions, and in the world to come, eternal life." Jesus said that we will have a hundredfold NOW in THIS time! Many of us will stop and go no further and never see the rest of the text. Again, I'm not saying that we're not to shout over this, but we need to understand that persecutions and trials will come. Jesus says to his disciples when speaking of the Holy Spirit:

John 16:1-4 (NCV)

> "I have told you these things to keep you from giving up. People will put you out of their synagogues. Yes, the time is coming when those who kill you will think they are offering service to God. They will do this because they have not known the Father, and they have not known me. I have told you these things now so that when the time comes, you will remember that

I warned you. "I did not tell you these things at the beginning because I was with you then.

Jesus tells them of the struggles that they will endure because of Him. There are many stories that I could present, but I think you get the picture by now. Jesus never sold us a fairytale. This is not to say that Christ doesn't care. He does; it's just that we must understand that trials will happen. Now we shouldn't walk around looking for the negative every day or expecting the worse. We should always enjoy the sunshine of good times and bask in the presence of good moments. However, for some of us, it's not that we're surprised by the misfortune of life; we may not know how to deal with it, and dealing with it requires us to face the disappointment.

Disappointments will attack three areas of our lives:

1) Our Christian Walk: I must not be saved because this happened (Don't become Job's friends)

2) Our Faith: I must not have faith because this happened

3) Does God Love Me? Is He really with me? I must have made God mad at me. I deserve this

Disappointments don't change the fact that you are a Christian. They don't mean that you don't have enough faith. And they definitely don't mean that God doesn't love you. On the contrary, you are being attacked because of these things. You are a Christian with faith in a God who loves you immensely. Also, remember, you're human.

When you don't handle disappointments properly, it will do one or two things:

1) You become like Naomi and change who you are

Ruth 1:20-21; 20 She said to them, "Do not call me Naomi (sweetness); call me Mara (bitter), for the Almighty has caused me great grief and bitterness. 21 I left full [with a husband and two sons], but the Lord has brought me back empty. Why call me Naomi, since the Lord has testified against me and the Almighty has afflicted me?"

Naomi had an unimaginable life-altering shift in her life. I can't even imagine losing a spouse but losing a spouse, and two children are beyond imaginable. When she returns home, she tells them not to call her Naomi but Mara, which means bitterness. Pain can shift your perspective on how you see yourself and how God sees you. In the moment of bitterness, you feel like God is punishing you, and it's His fault that this has happened. We naturally have to find a reason for our disappointments, and often, when we can't make sense of it, we say, "God is getting me back for what I did when I was thirteen." Disappointments in the hand of the enemy will always make you look bitter towards God and your life. Disappointment in the hand of God, although it's not easy, can refine you, define you, and strengthen you. The second thing that we do when we are disappointed is:

2) Shut off your ear toward God

Exodus 6:9 So Moses spoke thus to the children of Israel; but they did not heed Moses, because of anguish of spirit and cruel bondage.

One of the things that may cause loss of hearing or complications in hearing is head trauma. Since most of our thoughts, worries, anxiety, and pressure reside in our minds, disappointments can sometimes be head trauma. When we have so much happening at once or so many past disappointments, it makes it hard for us to hear, believe, and receive the promises of God. In the above scripture, God speaks to the children of Israel about their deliverance, but they can't accept it because of what they have endured in the past. We have often turned a deaf ear to God because of our anguish.

I love playing spades, and I love talking junk. I mean, slap the Joker on your forehead, junk. I remember playing with someone that said they could play, and when the game began, I soon realized that he couldn't play. I had some good hands, but my partner didn't know how to read the board, nor did he know how to bid. We got spanked; however, I still talked junk. After playing the game, a guy sat down and asked me to run with him. So I sat down and got dealt a garbage hand. I wanted to throw it back, but I had a face card, so I couldn't. My partner bid a ten, and I looked at him like, "Oh Lord, out the gate, we're going to lose." My mind was on my last partner, and I remembered he didn't know the game. However, this wasn't my previous partner, and I had to build trust in a new partner. We ran a Boston, and you better believe I talked major noise. I didn't have a good hand, but I pumped my partner up and just racked up the books he won. Notice that I didn't have a good hand, but I was still winning because of my partner. Sometimes in life, we're not dealt a good hand, but that doesn't mean we're going to lose. We have a partner in the Holy Spirit that holds all the trump cards, and we just have to rack up the books that He's winning because if He's winning, then we're winning. (If you don't know how to play spades, then I'm sorry for this analogy) My partner and I didn't get up for the rest of the night. Just like me, the children of Israel had some horrible partners in life that caused them to shut down when God showed up. Disappointments will make you think everyone is the same and no one can help you. You will then stay stuck in a place of bitterness and anger, but you don't have to wait there. It's okay to trust again because to deal with disappointments, you must trust your partner, Christ. Don't allow the failures of your last partner, or yourself, to cause you to throw in the towel on your life. Let's look at one more story. If there were someone in the Bible that I would never consider to have encountered a trial, it would be David. I mean, this man received the ultimate affirmation from God. God said, "This is a man after my OWN heart." Indeed God would protect him from any challenges. Nothing would come the way of this man. Right? Wrong. On the contrary, your position and title don't eliminate you from challenges. I remember growing up how I admired so many athletes; one, in particular, was Michael Jeffrey Jordan. I remembered trying to be like Mike. I watched him play, tried in every way, and failed horribly to emulate my game like his. I remember one morning waking up and getting ready for school; I saw on the news that his father had unfortunately died. My heart hurt for him and his family. At that moment, while watching him struggle for words to say at the podium, I realized that life could interrupt anyone. It doesn't matter your status. Death, sickness, bad news, etc., can come to any one of us. This is what happened to David. One day David and his men returned home to Ziklag only to find that the Amalekites had ravished his village. (1 Samuel 30:1-18) Before we discuss this, let's think about David's walking home from battle.

I'm sure he was happy that he hadn't lost a soldier in the war. All the men walked together with great joy and anticipation to return to their wives and children. I bet, even amid their fatigue, they could feel the embrace of their children in their arms. The vision of the smiles on their wives' faces once they returned burned within their minds. I can imagine that they rehearsed in their minds what they would say and the stories they would tell. However, to their surprise, they see smoke in the distance, and I can imagine them running to an unfamiliar village. No hugs from their children; they're gone. No stories to tell their wives; they're gone. No welcome-home parade but a welcome-home tragedy. Now their children's imagination has shifted from holding them in their arms to whether they will see them again. The thought of sharing a story with their companion is now, "Will I ever speak to them again?" The mental battles that occur when life interrupts our life are brutal. Grief sweeps in like an uncontrollable flood that has broken down our barrier of faith and trust, and we are now drowning in the flood of emotions, confusion, anger, and frustration.

"What do I do? What happened? Is God mad at me?" These are the questions that we ask ourselves when we encounter disappointments. What do you do when life hits you in an unexpected place? The first thing is that it's okay to cry. The Bible says that David and his men cried until there were no tears left to cry. These weren't wimpy men, nor were they cowardly men but men of great strength and valor, so for them to cry this intensely was a true sign of great distress and pain that they were feeling. There will, or may, come a tragedy that will cause the greatest Preacher, Psalmist, Teacher, Evangelist, etc., to fall to their knees in grief. These men experienced a state of misery that some of us experience, called shock. Shock is a response to something that has happened unexpectedly, good or bad. We love the shock of a new car, job promotion, wedding proposal, etc. This shock brings us tears of joy. However, the state of shock that these men felt didn't bring tears of joy but tears of anger, frustration, and pain. Their world has now been turned upside down, and everything in it has been stripped away. Out of their anger and frustration, they turned to blame David. When we face a tragedy in life, it's common to try and make sense of what just happened. In doing so, we often play the blame game. We either blame ourselves or someone else. They wanted to stone David because they felt that this was his fault. We often want to hurt people when we become hurt. We want others to feel the pain we're now experiencing, and these men wanted David to know their feeling. My good friend and great therapist, Shawndrika Cook, call this projected grief. David had lost his family just like theirs, but when you're angry, you don't care about anyone else's feelings but yours. But let's look at how David handled this:

1 Samuel 30:6 – Now David was greatly distressed, for the people spoke of stoning him because the soul of all the people was grieved, every man for his sons and daughters. But David strengthened himself in the Lord his God.

> *David didn't let allow what he felt to shift him.*

This verse states that David was greatly distressed because of what the people spoke of doing to him; however, David encouraged himself. Don't ever think that your words towards others don't affect them. David was distressed because of what they said of wanting to do to him. However, he didn't allow what he felt to shift him. He didn't let his army's anger toward him move his stance as a leader. He understood and took it; as a leader through hard times. You not only take the pain from the enemy but also from the very people you shepherd and love. Again, life will hurt, but don't allow what hurt you feel to shift you. The Bible says in Isaiah 54:17 that the weapon that's formed wouldn't prosper, but it NEVER said it wouldn't hurt. I spoke with a cop that had been shot while wearing a bulletproof vest. He told me that the vest stopped the bullet, but the bullet had left a deep tissue scar on his chest. God's grace and power can stop disappointments from prospering, but it still hurts and may leave scars. David, amid this pain, did something hard to do. He encouraged himself in the Lord. This scripture is often quoted as if David had wiped away all of his tears and gathered himself together. I don't see him that way. I believe he cried while encouraging himself. David hurt while encouraging himself. We have been taught that being tough and masculine is to wipe the tears from your face and act as if nothing has happened. We have been taught how to fake the appearance of being okay rather than becoming okay.

And guess what? It's okay not to be okay. Sometimes in life, you will have to become like David and learn to encourage yourself. However, you don't have to encourage yourself alone always. (We will discuss this a little later)

So How Do I deal with Disappointments?

Let me say that this is what helped me, so this isn't a concrete helping guide. One of these may help you or none, but I pray that one does.

1) Be honest before God

One thing we must understand is that God can handle your attitude. Your neck rolling will not offend Him. He will not destroy you for sharing how you feel. Ignoring your feelings doesn't make what you feel go away; it feeds it. Neglect is a Big Mac meal to frustration. Avoidance is the dessert that anxiety loves. We often don't know how to tell people how we feel, let alone God. I'm reminded of a story of a father who asked his son after seeing him come home frustrated, "Son, what's the problem?" The son responded, "It doesn't matter. No one cares." The father then tells his son, "I care, tell me about it." The son looks at his father with tears wailing up in his eyes and releases all of his frustration about life, school, relationships, and even his parents onto the father. The father asked him, "How do you feel now that you have released all of that?" The son said, "I feel better, but are you not mad?" The father says, "Sound wisdom can't be heard within the mind that's full of rage, hurt, confusion, and anger. I needed you to make room within your heart and mind for the answers that I'm about to give you because I was once there too." That's how our Heavenly Father responds to us. Release it on me so I can release My love and wisdom on you. Make room for what I'm about to pour out to you. Thomas Beckingham says, "At some point, the two worlds of whom we pretend to be and who we are must collide. It is, however, better to let those two worlds collide rather than have everything snap under the tension of keeping them apart." At some point, you'll have to get real before God. God can't produce a real deliverance until you give an honest confession. Psalm 62:8 "Trust in Him at all times, O people; pour out your hearts before Him. God is our refuge." Pour means it can't be controlled. Release it all before the Lord; believe me, He can handle it; you're the one who can't.

2) Don't stop praying (Pray in and through the frustration)

1 Samuel 1:10 – "Hannah was greatly distressed, and she prayed to the Lord and wept in anguish." Some of us pray when things are good or our favorite song is on. The

condition is just right. However, there will come a point in your life that your favorite song and prayer partner won't and can't help. The Bible says that Hannah was greatly distressed, but that didn't stop her from going to God in prayer. She wept while praying. She didn't wipe her face and gathered herself together. She cried before him while praying. Even Jesus wept at the tomb of Lazarus. We must not neglect our soul from expressing itself through tears. We are not beyond tears, and God knows this. He hears your silent prayers, and He sees your tears. God says to King Hezekiah, "I have heard your prayer; I have seen your tears" (2 Kings 20:5), and He's saying the same thing to you right now. You may weep, you may be in anguish, you may be in travail, but don't you STOP PRAYING. You will not wear God down with your consistent prayers. We must understand here that God may not always respond the way we want Him to, but He does respond in a place of concern. God hears your tears. Exodus 3:7-"Then the Lord said, "I have surely seen the affliction of my people who are in Egypt and have heard their cry because of their taskmasters. I know their sufferings." God has heard you and knows of your suffering, leading to the next step.

3) Trust God

Trusting God is hard because trusting God requires you to take your hands entirely off the situation and put your hands in His as He leads you through this journey. Joseph had to go through a pit, a dungeon, a prison, and then to a palace. He was trusting God while in pain can be challenging but not impossible. Trusting God in a place of uncertainty can be difficult but not impossible. A story that always baffled me in the Bible was when Peter and James went before Herod and James were beheaded before Peter and the people (Acts 12). Peter was told that he would be beheaded the next day, and he was thrown into a prison to await his death. What baffles me is when the angles come to WAKE HIM UP. Wait? WAKE HIM UP? Like, who goes to sleep after seeing their friend beheaded and awaiting your execution? However, when you trust God, you have an understanding and a peace that surpasses all understanding. I don't know how God will do this, but I trust Him. I don't see how God will get me out of this, but I trust Him. Disappointments can/will strip you of your rest. It will cause you to become anxious for God to move now and lose your confidence in His power. Peter went to sleep in prison, awaiting execution. Jesus went to sleep on a boat during a storm. David says, "When I am afraid, I put my trust in you" (Psalm 56:3). Let your response to fear be putting your trust in God. Be patient, and don't allow anxiety to push for something to change that you have no control over. This was me. I couldn't wait to get out of the hospital, and I had become impatient, which caused me to become restless and frustrated. However, I realized that my trust was in my expectation rather than Christ. Often, our expectations frustrate us, and when our expectations aren't met, we become frustrated and lose heart and faith. I had never been here before, so it required a new level of trust than I thought I had. I was afraid, but I put my trust in Him, and He made all things new in His time. The next chapter is one of the greatest choices that helped me.

"We must accept finite disappointment, but never lose infinite hope."

Martin Luther King Jr.

CHAPTER VIII
Get A Therapist

Proverbs 13:10 (b)
But with the well advised comes wisdom.

The mind is where everything begins and ends. It is our place of reasoning, consciousness, and where our emotions reside. When our minds are forever running, we only get sleep but no rest. You go to sleep, but you wake up tired from your mind running all night long. When your mind is clouded to the point that your reasoning is off, your consciousness has become unaware of your surroundings, and your emotions are all over the place, it may be a good idea to find a therapist. I remember coming home from the hospital. I was in a place of confusion and uncertainty. As I stated in the earlier chapters of this book, all I did was cry and wonder when life would return to normal. One of the things I've learned through this journey is that our expectations, when not met, lead us to a place of anger, frustration, or depression. Once I got home from the hospital, I expected things to return to the way they were, but none of that happened. I sat on the edge of my bed and just cried. I couldn't stop it, nor could I control it. Depression had set in, and hopelessness began to build in my mind. I tried to read the Bible, but I couldn't focus. I tried to pray, but tears became louder than my words. I remember laying in the bed while holding on to a pillow as a kid holding on to his stuffed animal during a storm, angry that what I was expecting wasn't happening. I felt like this was my life, and I was not okay with that. The problem was that I didn't know how to get out of this place, which clouded my thinking. Again, I prayed, read, walked, prayed some more, and instead of feeling better, I was still stuck in a place of hopelessness. However, my prayers were answered, just not how I thought they would be, but they were answered. My cousin Thandi Wells told me that I needed to get a therapist. I have never been against therapy, but I didn't think it would be the answer to my situation. Boy, was I wrong; it was exactly what I needed, and God knew it, and He sent me an amazing therapist. God answered my prayers through therapy. One thing we must understand about God is that He heals how He wants to heal. He may heal through a miracle, or He may heal through therapy. In the end, He does it because He's God. In the Bible, God healed seven blind men in seven different ways. We can never get to the place in life where we think we have figured God out. I'm reminded of a story that you may already know. There was a man who lived out in the country. A storm was on the horizon, and the people began to depart their homes and instructed the man that he should do the same. The man responded, "I'm going to stay here because God will take care of me." Sure enough, the storm came and flooded the man's house. This forced him to climb into the attic. As he sat in the attic, a lifeboat came, and the guard said, "Get on the boat; the waters are going to continue to get worse" the man replied, "I'm good; God is going to take care of me." The lifeboat departed, and sure enough, the waters began to rise, forcing the man to get to the roof of his now flooded home. He sat on his rooftop praying to God and believing for God to rescue him. At that moment, a rescue helicopter flew over him and yelled, "Get on, the flood is going to get worse," yet the man replied, "God is going to save me." The helicopter flew away, and unfortunately, the man drowned. When the man got to Heaven, he was very disappointed in God and asked Him, "Why didn't you save me?" God replied, "I sent you warnings from your neighbor, a lifeboat, and a helicopter; what else could I do for you?"

I may not have told that story accurately, but I hope you get the point. God's methods are forever changing, and we must know what He's sending to help us. I know many people have this stigma of therapists: all they want is your money. But let me help you understand something. You're spending all your money on food because you're eating emotionally to hide your problem. You're spending all your money on alcohol because you're trying to drink away your problem. You're spending money on clothes because you've become an emotional shopper, and you're trying dress up (cover up) your problems. You may run to sex, porn, the corner of a dark room, pain killers, sleep, etc. and

> *God uses a therapist as a lifeboat to help guide you out of the attic of your mind.*

none of these things work. Instead of these things working, you become dependent on these things to help you cope. And that's the problem; you're coping with the problem and not dealing with the problem. A therapist doesn't help you become dependent upon them, nor do they teach you to simply cope with life, but how to overcome it. God uses a therapist, just like the story I shared, as a lifeboat to help guide you out of the attic of your mind or as a helicopter to help lift you from the rooftop of your emotions. Therapists will lead you to solutions, as what methods you choose to cope with leads to addiction. I remember sitting out in the parking lot waiting to go in for my first visit with my therapist, and I sat there wondering if this would work. Once I was called back, it wasn't a second into the conversation that I was in tears. I opened up about my story, and he helped me understand the grief process and how to develop strategies for dealing with my new norm. My new norm? This was a question that I asked myself because I didn't want a new norm; I wanted my old norm. However, my new norm wasn't going anywhere. My therapist is a retired Pastor, a believer in Christ, and someone who understood the battle of life both physically and spiritually, and he has been a guide ever since. He helped me deal with the insecurities of being a husband who now needed my wife's help and a pastor who feared losing his church. So the questions I'm asked quite often are: "Why did you get a therapist?" "Aren't you a

Pastor?" "Don't you have enough faith in God to believe that He will make it better?" These questions come because I am very open and honest about my physical and mental health. I have shared my story with numerous people, and when I get to the therapist part, the people I'm speaking with begin to shy away. I get it. Growing up in my generation, every household held the same code; what goes on here stays here. We were told never to share our issues or struggles with anyone outside our home. Even when we got to school, and the school counselor asked how are things going, we were conditioned to answer the same general answer, "I'm fine," when in reality, we weren't. You were taught to tough it out if you got hurt if you played sports. Most men had fathers who they never saw cry nor heard them open up about life. Fathers taught their sons to be tough; unfortunately, their definition of tough consisted of showing no weakness, no tears, just blood, sweat, and perseverance. We have been taught to struggle in silence. We have been conditioned not to allow anyone in the room of our heart where brokenness, bitterness, and confusion resides. Some people found comfort at the bottom of a bottle or blowing smoke in the atmosphere. However, this doesn't alleviate the pain. Lying to yourself doesn't negate the reality of the struggle that you are facing. The only thing avoidance does is grow your struggle, but it won't control or alleviate it. This is why you may become angry towards life and people. So why did I get a therapist? Because throughout my life, I had struggles and battles that I didn't know how to handle or deal with. Silence and a fake smile became my go-to mechanism. However, a battle in your life will come that you may need help with to guide you. And this is what my therapist did for me.

Understanding Therapy

Most of us run from therapy because of what I just stated above. However, a vast majority run from therapists because they don't understand what therapy is. People have watched T.V. shows and movies and seen where the person sits on a couch and pours out to someone who could honestly care less about what they are saying. This is far from the truth. Therapy is there to help you with your mental. We have doctors, nurse practitioners, and nurses for our physical state, and we have the same for our mental. The Bible teaches us to serve the Lord with our mind, body, and soul. We take good care of our bodies. We look out for our souls. However, when it comes to our minds that is something we often neglect. Mental health is real, and mental health, when not dealt with properly, can lead to some horrible places in your life. You become socially distant when you once were the life of the party. You become distant from everyday activities. You may lose your motivation to move, want to sleep more than usual, and become overwhelmed by the stress of your current situation. Mental health issues can affect your relationships with your loved ones, job, marriage, emotions, self-esteem, etc. Low self-esteem had become a problem for me because having had a womb vac and colostomy bag on my stomach left a huge scar on my body that I didn't want my wife to see. My scar made me very self-conscious. Although no one could see my stomach, I knew what it looked like, and I didn't want to go out in public because it was a challenge. Again, this was my new norm, and my therapist taught me how to deal with it. Getting a therapist doesn't mean that you are belittling your faith in God. Do you feel that way when you go to your foot doctor or a specialist? Then why do you feel the need to question your faith when going to see a therapist? It's okay. I promise you. A therapist is there to help guide you through the mental challenges you are facing. I remember sharing things with my therapist that weren't even in my current state. It was things from my youth that had somehow found their way back into my mind. Therapy will make you face some things you may not want to face but need to address. This is another reason that some may not want to go to therapy because they feel it's no need to relive or deal with those moments. A good therapist will not make you rush into a place you don't want to visit, but they are trained to help guide you through and conquer those past giants. I learned more about myself through counseling that I didn't know was a part of me and habits that formed as defense mechanisms to avoid the challenges of the moment. Another thing about therapy is that it is not a magic pill. It doesn't fix everything at that moment. Just like it takes broken legs months to heal, it may take you the same time to heal mental brokenness. However, don't get discouraged by that. When people go on a diet, they want to see the weight fall off right then, but we know it doesn't happen like that. Some will become upset that they don't see the results of the weight within two weeks, but they fail to recognize that they're not as tired as they once were. They are healthier because of their food choices, and their strength is returning. Why do I say this? Some results in therapy may not always be visual; if you're not careful, your expectations will have you missing the small victories. You're now walking through the grocery store and not worrying. You've now driven to the park and sat in your car instead of being cooped up in your bedroom. Small victories! It's hard to see those victories and celebrate those victories when you keep focusing on your overall battle. There's an old saying that the way you eat an elephant is one bite at a time. Celebrate the small victories. A mind and heart that are not healed are like poison to every positive thing in your life. It won't allow you to see or enjoy the good moments and days. I had to learn how to see the good in my own life. I had become so negative toward my situation that I couldn't see the Hand of God on my life.

I would go to the park, sit on the benches, and watch the birds. However, I would get mad because I wanted to walk like everyone else. I had lost the view of the good moment of actually being out of the house and being and out and about. I couldn't celebrate that because I had become angry at being too tired to walk. The next day I made up my mind that I would go and walk the entire track. Well, that didn't happen. I barely made it across the bridge. I didn't realize that the day before, I could barely move, and this day I'm walking. I was making progress, but the bitterness was stripping me from seeing progress. All I saw was my expectations not being met. I would love to say that I learned how to celebrate those moments alone, but nope, my therapist brought those victories to my attention. Now I hear some of you saying, "I already know how to do that, so I am good." I celebrate you, my friend. This chapter may not be for you. I knew these things too. The problem was that I knew it for others and not for myself. I knew how to encourage and build up everyone else, but not me. I needed that understanding in this battle. I didn't realize that I had become my biggest stumbling block. I hadn't accepted the fact that my life had forever changed. I was able to bounce back from Cancer 11 years ago, but this battle was different. I thought I would pop back up as I did then, but I'm not as youthful as I was then. A story that I love is the one with the 3 Hebrew boys. If their attention remained on the fire, they would have never had the opportunity to see Jesus in the fire with them. Sometimes we need help taking our eyes off the

> *Christ not only sees your smile but your tears as well*

fire and seeing Christ in the fire of life with us. I had to realize that Christ was with me on the days that I could hardly move and that I felt like Super Man. Christ not only sees your smile but your tears as well. Now, making that statement may have triggered the million-dollar question. "Well, if God is with me, why didn't he stop this from happening?" As a Pastor, I have heard and asked this question a million times. This is one of the most challenging questions to answer because ten times out of ten, it's coming from a raw place of hurt and emotions. We're just trying to make sense of our current circumstances. We're trying to figure out why has my life become interrupted? And this, my friend, is why you need a good pastor who understands that for you to make sense of your situation right now, you may need a therapist. In conclusion, to this chapter, please know that I don't consider myself an expert in this area. I am just one of those pastors that understands that I don't have all the answers to everyone's problems, and we as Pastors need to know that. I am not trained to handle molestation, rape, murder, unexpected death, trauma, etc. The scripture above states, "With the well advised comes Wisdom," and I want everyone connected to me or reading this book to receive wisdom through the guidance they may receive outside of my council. Proverbs 15:22 "Plans fail without advice, but with many counselors they are confirmed."

What to look for in a Counselor/Therapist

In our church, I have different therapists to come in and talk to my church as a whole or directly to my leaders quarterly. In one session, my good friend, LPC Shawndrika Cook of Cultivation Center, came in and talked to my leaders. One of the things that she brought up that I would like to share is how to find a good therapist. She mentioned questions to ask when looking for a therapist:

1) What's their availability?

2) Do they do free consultation?

3) What are the prices?

4) Do they charge by the hour or the session?

But the last one that she gave was good.

5) What's their level of Christianity (If looking for a Christian Counselor)

You want to make sure that you find a therapist that has your beliefs if you are a believer. Because, if you go to a therapist that doesn't believe in God and you go in and tell them that you are talking to God, well, don't be surprised if they write you down as having Schizophrenia because you're talking to someone that they don't believe is there. Don't be afraid to ask questions about who you're going to. Don't allow people to throw you into sessions with people that don't have the same level of faith or understanding. Now with that being said. I praise God that my therapist is a retired pastor and a true believer; however, he doesn't preach to me as a pastoral counselor. Going to a Christian therapist doesn't mean that they are going to preach to you the entire session or at all. They may add biblical references in their counseling to help you understand, but they will also keep it real with you and not make everything so spiritual. Not saying that it's a bad thing, but sometimes we as believers can overly spiritualize things and need to be pulled back into reality. I do this even as a pastor who counsels.

"It's okay to have Jesus and a Therapist."

Dr. Maurice Valentine

CHAPTER IX
Live Again

New beginnings or starting over is often disguised as a painful or failed ending.

Lao Tzu

One challenge about coming out of a traumatizing experience is learning how to live again. Or start over. Is it possible? Can I do this? Will something else happen again? All these questions run through our minds as we think about moving on with life. Peter had this mindset in the story of Jesus telling him to launch his net out for a great catch in Luke 5:1-7. Peter didn't jump for joy at Jesus' request, nor was he excited to throw his nets back into the water. Why? Because Peter had fished the night before and caught nothing, and that's where his mind was, on the nothing he had caught. He had washed his nets, ready to go home to a warm bed, and here comes this man, getting in his boat and telling him to launch into the deep. Peter knew the work that he had just put into cleaning those nets. Cleaning nets that have caught something is much easier and more exciting than cleaning nets that have caught nothing. That's how our outlook on life could be after experiencing a life-altering moment. We remember the negative parts of the experience, making us hesitant to cast our nets back into the sea of life. We remember that pain of losing, so we're afraid to love again. Peter had a change of heart, though. He thought about his statement and Jesus' request. Jesus will never ask you to do something again that will bring you more disappointment. Peter told Jesus we've been out here all night and caught nothing. It would have been different if they were in another lake. But they were in the same lake that he was in the night before, and sometimes when you're in the same place within life, it's hard to believe that things can change. Because this is the same lake, I don't believe I will catch anything. When God asks you to do something in the same location, He's trying to elevate your faith in a place where you've fallen. Peter had to choose between his doubts and Jesus' words. He chose the word and launched out into the sea (Luke 5:4-7). He caught so many fish that he had to signal to his friends to come and help him. Question? What if he had followed his fear to launch out? Would he have caught anything? Would his friends and family have benefited from his fear of catching nothing? No, they wouldn't have. And guess what? Neither will you nor your family benefit from you holding on to your net of life. I understand that your trauma was trauma, and it was more traumatizing than not catching any fish. I'm sure you would have wanted that over whatever battle you have faced. However, you're not throwing your net out there to catch fish. You're throwing your net out to catch a break. This is the saying that we often say when facing trial after trial, "Man, I can't catch a break!" Well, if you throw back out there, I believe this time, you will. It's hard to forget what you've gone through or currently going through. Whatever it was challenged your faith, family, mind, and soul, but if you're not careful, you may find yourself speaking negatively over yourself and accepting what is to be the rest of your life. God says in Isaiah 43:18-19, "Behold, I am doing a new thing." I'm going to stop right there because this is important to know. God made a statement that I believe we should all hear. I knew I needed to hear it when battling my situation, which is, "BEHOLD." This means changing what you're looking at and shifting your vision.

> *What you focus on becomes you!*

Behold, your new mind. Behold, your new life. Behold your joy, peace, and happiness. BEHOLD! LOOK! LOOK AT WHAT I AM DOING! We have difficulty shifting our focus from trauma to triumph, disappointment to happiness, victim to victory, etc. What you focus on becomes YOU! To live again, you have to look not at what happened to you but at what happened for you. Please hear me. I do not want to downplay what you've gone through. Did it hurt? Yes. But shifting your focus is not forgetting what happened to you but getting free from the power of what happened to you. It will not control you, nor will it dictate your life. So this is why God says, "BEHOLD" in this scripture because of where their attention was. Let's read the verse in its entirety: Isaiah 43:18-19 (NKJV) "Remember not the former things, nor consider the things of old. Behold, I am doing a new thing; now it springs forth, do you not perceive it? I will make a way in the wilderness and rivers in the desert. God says, "Remember not the former things nor consider the things of old." This is why God says BEHOLD because our eyes are on our past trauma or mistakes. Peter's mind was on the failure of the night before. God tells us not to remember. Again, this doesn't mean you will forget what happened to you; it means letting go of your past's power.

I will never forget the hospital and operating rooms I was in for what felt like years. However, the fear of those rooms was strong at one point, but they are gone now. The fear of walking back into that hospital is gone because I had to do it while visiting my sister. Something that's crazy, my sister had a small procedure done, and she wanted me to go to the hospital with her, and the same holding room they put me in when I was going through my battle was the same one they had her in. The nurses even remembered me. I didn't want to go back in there. I didn't think I was ready, but I had to launch my net and live. I couldn't let the fear of that hospital keep me away from my family. Did I remember the pain, anxiety, and depression in that room? Yes! Did It bring fear to my heart, mind, and soul? No! I took power away from those memories because I chose to "BEHOLD" what God was doing. That visit did more for me than it did for my sister. Every inch of that hospital brought fear to me. The memory of it had me paralyzed at times. But I chose to BEHOLD. It took me a minute, some prayer, God, and a few therapy sessions, but I got over it. God was doing a new thing within me. He was making me stronger than in my past. I was David, and that hospital had become my Goliath, and by His might, I slayed it and took the head with me as a reminder to "BEHOLD." And you will do the same, my friend! It's not easy to face your past, but it is possible. My Spiritual Grandfather, Apostle Maurice K. Wright, used to preach, "No confrontation, No Resolution." God will give you Supernatural strength to face your giants and snatch away the power of your past. Your past will become a testimony and no longer trauma. Facing your giants won't always be in an ideal environment. We often wait or pray for the condition of our life to be right before we try to change our minds and hearts. However, God doesn't need perfect conditions to show up and create new things. Remember the Spirit of God hovered over the earth when it was dark and void (Genesis 1:2). God created the universe out of nothing, and He can do the same with us. Notice the condition in which God said He would do a new thing: "I will make a way in the Wilderness, and I will make rivers in the Desert." A wilderness is where things have grown, but it hasn't been cultivated nor taken care of, like your joy, peace, health, and life. You have life; it's just all over the place. You have joy but can't find it because it's hidden behind the wild bushes of doubt and anxiety. However, God said, "I will make a way through all of that." There is nothing too wild that God can't get through to get to you. He has gotten through the briers of your past, the shrubs of your fear, and the many venomous doubts that love to rest under the shade of fear. Here's the challenging factor. God said He would make a way; the question is, will you get up and walk on the way He has made for you to live again. We must decide to get out of the jungle of our minds, step out of our pasts and into our lives, and LIVE AGAIN! You can get up, my friend. With tears in your eyes, get up. I know your heart may be heavy, but get up. Have you ever seen a house that hasn't been kept for years? I don't care how nice the neighborhood is; if that house isn't taken care of, the elements will soon take over. The vines will cover the windows and the grass will consume the sidewalk. Well, this happens to your mind if you don't GET UP. If you sit there, the wild thoughts will consume you, and you will begin not just to think but to believe that this is the way life is supposed to be. NO! GET UP! Get on the path to your new life and freedom. Let's look at the other place where God said He would move. A desert is a bit different from the wilderness. The wilderness is a place where there's wild growth. On the other hand, the desert has no growth, only dry places, and desolation. The desert is that person that has no hope, no joy, no peace, no anything. They are just existing. Nothing is growing for them, and nothing is flowing for them. Every time something good comes along, the heat of life dries it up. There's nothing to pull from, nor a resource to return to for support. Until now! What I love about God is that He is the resource we can pull from. For there to be rivers in a desert, there have to be two things. Number one; a downpour. This happens when there's a great outpouring from a storm. Sometimes in life, our storms can be our water source. We never know how God chooses to supply all of our needs. Why does it feel that it keeps raining in my life? Maybe, this storm is providing an overflow in your life, but can you see it? The second one is what I choose that provides water, and I believe that God spoke of this one because it's a miracle of the two events. There has to be another water source for the desert to pull from, and what do you know, Jesus is that source. John 4:14- But whoever drinks the water I give him will never thirst. Indeed, the water I give him will become in him a fount of water springing up to eternal life." He is the source that can make a dry life come to life. To this day, I still have moments of PTSD, but it's within those moments that His life springs into action, and I sit back and "BEHOLD." I take my eyes off of what was and put them onto what is now. God can do it. Again, I can't say when but I promise you; it will get better, my friend. You can and will live again. You have more chapters in your life, my friend. Don't allow this one chapter to define you in your walk with Christ. It hurt you. It scared you. It may have even crippled you. But it didn't destroy you. They didn't destroy you. God did not keep you on this earth to be tortured by trauma. You are here to tell your story about how you made it over and conquered your battle. The enemy tries to use depression to shut up your mouth. He doesn't want your story to get out. I learned of a message about depression: "If you rearrange the letters in depression, it spells the phrase I PRESSED ON." And that's exactly the story he doesn't want you to tell. You Pressed On! Paul Says in Philippians 3:12, "Not that I have already attained, or am already perfected; but I PRESS on, that I may lay hold of that which is Christ Jesus has also laid hold of me." The definition of the word press means to move into contact with, and that's what Paul had a mind to do, and we must also develop that mindset. I will not stop pressing until I come into contact with what I'm pressing to reach. You are pressing for your life; don't stop until you come into contact with it! With tears in your eyes, press on. Like the late great

> *With tears in your eyes, press on!*

Dr. Mya Angelou says, "But still, I Rise." Christ got up with nail prints in his hands and feet. He probably still had scars from the beating He took and prints on His forehead. However, Christ didn't look at His scars and allow that to keep Him in the grave. I hear you, "But I'm not Christ." That's true, but the same Spirit that raised Him from the grave now resides in you if you are a believer (Romans 6:10-11). Now, you're okay if you haven't believed in Christ or something pulled you away from His love. He's not mad at you, but He's madly in love with you. Just repeat after me, "Lord, I believe you sent your only Son to earth to die for my sins. I believe He died and rose three days later, freeing me from a life of sin, and has now given me the right to call you My Father. I give you my life and open my heart to receive your Holy Spirit to help me walk this believer's walk of faith. In Jesus' name, Amen." Welcome to the family if you prayed that prayer. We love you and thank God for you. If you didn't pray that prayer, we still love you and thank God for you. You can live again, and I pray you choose to do so. No, it's not easy, but, again, you can do it. I would love to leave you some things that may help you to live again.

1) Find a Church Home

It's important to find a place of worship that can feed you and strengthen you through the word of God. A place with great singing and music is good, but a place of teaching and understanding is better. You need a place to go where it's okay to ask questions and inquire about where you may be spiritually. A ministry that can help guide you on your journey of conquering.

2) Find you a strong support/accountability group

This doesn't have to be a big group. It should include mature Christians, church members, or friends. If you are an introvert, that's cool; start with one. Talk to this person, explain to them where you are mentally, and trust them to guide you back on the path of victory when/if you step off.

3) Find you a Therapist

I know by now you probably think this is a book to help you get a therapist. If you need one, then it is. As I stated in the eighth chapter, a therapist is just someone to guide you through the unknown terrain of life at this moment. Your accountability group, or person, is the person that you can call morning, noon, and night. Some therapists won't allow that, and that's okay. They do have a life too. We don't need a What About Bob moment happening. (If you don't know what that movie is; it's CLASSIC)

4) Find an activity

Try new things. Find something that interests you and allows you to use the creative side of your mind more and creates the serotonin of happiness within your body and mind. Go walking, fishing, bird watching (My New Favorite Hobby), cruising down the highway with the windows open on a beautiful day. Whatever brings you peace, do it, my friend. Skip a rock on the lake. Throw some ribs on the grill. Just do whatever puts a smile on your face.

5) Be Patient With yourself

Don't be so hard on yourself. You may have just come out of a traumatic situation, and it's going to take small steps to get up. An acronym the Lord gave me for small was S.M.A.L.L. (Seeing Major Accomplishments Little by Little). What's a major accomplishment? A few are getting up, walking, sitting outside, combing your hair, and even going to the grocery store. When you can do what you struggled to do before, that's major. I hear you, "Well, I once upon a time could walk five miles and not get tired." That was then; this is now, and the five steps you just took are MAJOR! Give yourself some grace and congratulate yourself on the small things.

Live Again!

"Everything negative - pressure, challenges - is all an opportunity for me to rise."

Kobe Bryant

ABOUT THE AUTHOR

Dr. Maurice Valentine is the Pastor and founder of Life Changing Christian Center. He is a lover of God's people and has a desire to see them grow and flourish in their purpose in life. Valentine's passion for people is often revealed as he diligently works to help others navigate the challenges in their daily walks. As a Cancer survivor and health advocate, he has found a targeted devotion toward assisting those in difficult health crises like that he endured in managing the pain of Diverticulitis. He holds an earned Doctor of Theology (Th.D.) degree and leads a generation of church leaders to achieve their educational goals by overseeing a satellite location of a College of Theology located at Life Changing Christian Center in Pelham, Alabama. He is honored to share his life with his wife and best friend, Salisia Valentine, with whom he partners to inspire God's people through biblical truths and expressions of the Love of Jesus Christ.

Connect with Dr. Valentine

www.MauriceCValentine.com

www.ingramcontent.com/pod-product-compliance
Lightning Source LLC
Chambersburg PA
CBHW071433080526
44587CB00014B/1831